*For Alexander*

# London: the promised land?

## The Migrant Experience in a Capital City

*Edited by*
ANNE J. KERSHEN

Published on behalf of the Centre for the Study of Migration

**Avebury**
Aldershot • Brookfield USA • Hong Kong • Singapore • Sydney

Published by
Avebury
Ashgate Publishing Limited
Gower House
Croft Road
Aldershot
Hants GU11 3HR
England

Ashgate Publishing Company
Old Post Road
Brookfield
Vermont 05036
USA

**British Library Cataloguing in Publication Data**
London : the promised land?
1. London (England) - Emigration and immigration
I.Kershen, Anne J., 1942 -
304.8'421

**Library of Congress Catalog Card Number:** 96-080382

ISBN 1 85972 630 5

Printed and bound by Athenaeum Press, Ltd.,
Gateshead, Tyne & Wear.

# Contents

# Contributors

**John Eade** is Principal Lecturer in the Department of Sociology and Social Policy at the Roehampton Institute, London. He has published numerous articles and chapters on Bangladeshis in Britain, particularly in Tower Hamlets, and published a book, *The Politics of Community: The Bangladeshi Community in East London.* He has undertaken research in Calcutta concerning the Bengali Muslim middle class and has written about pilgrimage and tourism, co-editing with Michael Sallnow, *Contesting the Sacred: The Anthropology of Christian Pilgrimage*. He has also edited *Living the Global City*: *Globalization a Local Process* (1997).

**Mike Fenton** is Manager, Local Economy Policy Unit (LEPU), South Bank University. He has had a long-term interest in location patterns of minority ethnic groups and was Research Associate at the SSRC Research Unit on Ethnic Relations. He has published widely on matters related to local economic development. He has directed a wide range of research projects on urban regeneration and local economies and is currently engaged in evaluating the Bethnal Green City Challenge programme.

**William J. Fishman** was formerly Senior Research Fellow, with special reference to the social history and politics of East London, and is now Visiting Professor, in the Department of Political Studies at Queen Mary and Westfield College, University of London. His publications include *The Insurrectionists* (1970), *East End Jewish Radicals* (1975), *The*

*Streets of East London* (1979), *East End 1888* (1988) plus numerous contributory articles and reviews. He is currently working on *Into the Abyss: a Duo of Victorians, W.T. Stead and E.R. Sims*, exploring the 'underclass' of London.

**Andrew Godley** is a lecturer in Economics at the University of Reading. He has published a number of papers related to his prize-winning Ph.D thesis in journals such as *Journal of Economic History*, *Business History* and *Textile History*. He has also edited collections on *Business History and Business Culture* (1996) and *Banks, Networks and Venture Capital* (1996).

**Colin Holmes** is a Professor of History in the University of Sheffield. He is the author of *Anti-Semitism in British Society 1879-1939* (1979), *John Bull's Island* (1988) and *A Tolerant Country?* (1991). He is also the editor of a number of collections, as well as being the joint editor of the journal, *Immigrants and Minorities*.

**Anne J. Kershen** is Barnett Shine Senior Research Fellow and Director of the Centre for the Study of Migration, at Queen Mary and Westfield College. She is the author of *Uniting the Tailors* (1995), and co-author of *Tradition & Change: A History of Reform Judaism in Britain 1840.* She has contributed chapters to *The Making of Modern Anglo-Jewry* (1990), *Outsiders and Outcasts* (1993) and *The Peopling of London* (1993). She is currently working on a study of East London which explores its influence on national politics and events over the past one hundred and fifty years.

**Philip Nanton** is an Associate Fellow in the Centre of West African Studies in the University of Birmingham. He has lectured in Applied Social Policy in the Department of Local Government Studies. He has published in the field of public policy, race relations and equal opportunities and is currently researching aspects of Caribbean migration.

**Stanley Waterman** is Professor of Geography in the University of Haifa. He has published papers on electoral reform in Israel, the non-Jewish vote in Israel in 1992, spatial separation and boundaries, partition, secession and peace in our time and, with Marlena Schmool, the Jewish immigrant experience in Britain. He is currently working on *Carnivals for Elites: The Cultural Politics of Arts Festivals* and *Spatial Separation and Human Geography: A Study of Division, Segregation and Partition.*

# Preface

The Centre for the Study of Migration was established in the autumn of 1994 at Queen Mary and Westfield College, University of London, in order to provide a focal point in London for those concerned with the study of the movements of people locally, nationally and internationally. QMW is located in the East End of London, an area which for hundreds of years has been the first place of settlement for immigrants and an entry point for those outside the capital who sought their future within its walls. It provides a natural home for a Centre which has made the diverse facets of migration its *raison d'être*. The Centre is inter-disciplinary and is supported by a Steering Committee composed of representatives from the College's Departments of Economics, English, French, Geography, History, Medical Science and Political Studies. It pursues a policy of initiating and encouraging research and providing a programme of seminars, conferences and publications.

In November 1995 the Centre held its official launch Conference on the theme of *London: A Promised Land?* Although the Centre is not Metrocentric it was thought fitting that its first activity should concentrate on, indeed celebrate, a city that, for almost two thousand years, has been no stranger to the influences and contributions of migrants from other areas, cities, countries and continents. This volume is a collection of papers given at that Conference plus additions which expand on the theme. Future volumes are scheduled to follow. These will have a much stronger international content and will reflect the diversity of interests and disciplines engaged in the field of migration studies as we enter the twenty-first century.

I should like to express my gratitude to those who have contributed to this volume and who have stoically tolerated my letters, faxes and phone calls with requests for manuscript delivery. I should also like to thank the members of the Centre's Steering Committee for their input and support, Professor Philip Ogden for co-chairing the first Conference, my colleagues in the Department of Political Studies at Queen Mary and Westfield College, the Departmental Secretary Jasmine Salucideen for secretarial and administrative help, Jay, Brian and Francois of the Arts Faculty Computer Services Department, the staff of QMW library, especially Eilis Rafferty and Chris Lloyd of Tower Hamlets Local History Library. My most particular thanks to Professor Ken Young for his support throughout the creation and establishment of the Centre and with the preparation of this volume. His help at all times has been invaluable. Finally, my thanks to my husband and family for their forbearance during the preparation of this volume.

Anne J. Kershen
Director, Centre for the Study of Migration
Queen Mary and Westfield College
Autumn 1996

# 1 Introduction

*Anne J. Kershen*

The movement of peoples is as old as the Bible. Whilst the Hebrews were searching for the 'land flowing with milk and honey',[1] Hittites and Kassites were on the move; in later centuries the Romans, Goths and Mongols also crossed geographic and territorial boundaries. All were looking for 'the promised land', though its form differed from group to group. Some sought a peaceful haven, others land and its natives to subordinate. Migrants have not always found their utopia, many have had to work at creating it. The successful being those who, in Machiavellian fashion, recognised the potential and used initiative and ability to create good fortune.

There is no one theory which satisfactorily accounts for the various patterns of migration that have taken place over the centuries. The 'push and pull'[2] factor is an old faithful which proposes that dissatisfaction with the native environment is matched by the attraction of *elsewhere*; thus is created the immigrant, a more or less willing traveller seeking economic advancement in the next village, state, country or continent. In the nineteenth century eastern European Jews moved westwards to Britain and America. The majority left the Pale of Settlement, not simply to escape the pogroms,[3] but in search of economic opportunity in cities 'paved with gold'. Many of those who travelled from the Caribbean Islands in the mid-1950s did so to escape both growing unemployment at home and to fill job vacancies in Britain. In a global world intercontinental migration is no longer a dream but a reality available to even the most distant Sylheti villager - though often the dream can become a nightmare. Little push and lots of pull leads us to another theory, that of the carrot of riches or enhanced opportunity. The Norman dukes followed William the Conqueror because they thought, rightly, that England under the Norman King offered far more than northern France, whilst bankers from Lombardy eagerly took the place of the expelled Jews after 1290. Today, national newspaper and property magnates cross continents and become 'tycoon migrants' in order to expand their empires.

Not all migrations were willing. Some individuals and groups were moved by physical force in the name of empire building. The Romans transported their slaves across oceans and mountains, whilst from the sixteenth century onwards, 'European mercantilism initiated the largest process of forced migration...ten million slaves from Western Africa to the New World'.[4] Somewhere in between 'voluntary' and 'slavery' is 'indentured', a system whereby those with no expectations of economic mobility at home contracted themselves to become, what in many instances proved to be, little more than slaves.[5] More recently, sojourners, looking only to spend a short while in a city or a country in order to acquire capital sufficient to allow them to return home as 'rich men of status',[6] have found themselves trapped. Events taking place on the broader canvas enforced an extended stay, which for many has become permanent. Has this given rise to a new concept, that of the 'on the spot' creation of the promised land? If this is so, is it one which embraces the culture and practices of home, an incorporation of the new and the old and or an ideal born out of the actual experience of migration and settlement? The late twentieth century global economy has produced labour migrants, a condition where 'choice of residence accompanies change of job'.[7] This in turn has given birth to the relocation industry; individuals or groups moved by the company, for the company to a destination chosen by the company.

Willing but needy economic migrants, fortune seekers, forced labour, sojourners turned immigrants, labour migrants and, finally, those seeking refuge. The Huguenots fled from religious oppression in the seventeenth century; two hundred years later radical intellectuals, from eastern and central Europe, sought freedom of political expression; others have been refugees fleeing from military oppression and dictatorships which demanded an individual's soul as well as his body. In the inter-war years refugees from Nazism pleaded for entry into countries less tolerant than in earlier times:[8] internal political upheavals during the second half of the twentieth century have led to a dramatic increase in numbers of asylum seekers. Now, as the century draws to its close, many would-be immigrants are forced to become illegal entrants, using hidden routes into countries whose policies have been to systematically tighten their immigration laws.[9]

Before examining the reasons why London has been the first point of settlement for the different groups referred to in this volume, it is important to stress that any analysis of the migrant experience, be it short or long stay, has to be viewed within a wide framework. The roots of the migrant group in terms of native economy, family structure, the role of religion, kinship and village relationships, are all tools to be used in the learning process which enables us to comprehend cause and effect in the various stages of migration. Having reached that point on the chart we can then begin to evaluate the qualities looked for in the promised land and consider what concessions and contributions have been, and need to be, made in order to achieve the dream. One further point, whilst conclusions can be drawn as to the totality of the migrant experience - in the sense of regional mobility, return or onward migration - for those who settled in London some 150 years ago, it is impossible to do the same with more recent arrivals. In the pages that follow John Eade, Mike Fenton, Anne Kershen, Philip Nanton and Stanley Waterman illustrate that regional migration, secondary migration, return migration and re-migration, are characteristics of the post-modern world. The conclusions about today's migrants will have to wait until well into the 21st century.

**Why London?**

The Romans liked their location on the Thames so well, they stayed, walled it and called it Londinium. In the centuries that followed, from beyond its protected boundary, London was perceived as the Promised Land, drawing an almost unceasing inward flow of migrants[10] to the capital of a nation which, by the late nineteenth century, had gained the reputation as the most tolerant in the civilised world. A title which Colin Holmes suggests is now open to question.[11]

The contributions that follow provide us with a number of answers to the question, *why London?* Over the centuries the commonest denominator has been perceived, and real, economic opportunity, albeit at different levels and with varying expectations. Holmes provides us with a fascinating mosaic of those who have sought - and the smaller number who have made

- London their base for financial and social success. William Fishman describes how Irish labour was drawn to London's streets and docks for 'a roof and a livelihood'. Kershen illustrates how the Calvinist Huguenots combined the Protestant work ethic with economic opportunity in the silk trade, whilst Fishman, Andrew Godley, Holmes and Kershen all use the Jewish experience to provide examples of the way in which news of London's burgeoning nineteenth century tailoring trade found its way to the *stetls* and towns of eastern Europe. Eade, Fenton, Holmes and Kershen describe how, in more recent years, people from what was originally the north eastern corner of India, subsequently Pakistan and now Bangladesh, used the Empire connection to find their way to, and work in, the streets of East London. Nanton provides an example of another Empire connection when writing about the entry of people from the Caribbean islands after the Second World War. Empire and industry, the combination of the two in an economic context providing one of the major reasons why Britain, and thus, London was perceived as the promised land.

Empire and hope of employment were not the only reasons why London was chosen. Eade, Kershen and Nanton, illustrate the way in which direct labour recruitment has to be seen as a major factor in the arrival of immigrants to our shores. Whilst it is well-known that Chinese seamen and lascars were recruited in the nineteenth century and that London Transport, ethnic restaurants, textile and clothing factories recruited overseas labour after the Second World War, it is perhaps less well known that some immigrant eastern European workshop masters looked directly to the sweatshops of Russia and Poland for their work force in the 1870s.[12]

During the nineteenth century Britain operated an open door policy towards immigrants. Unlike other European nations, and America after 1882,[13] only criminals, lunatics and the contagiously sick were excluded. Reference has already been made to the attraction of London for political and religious dissidents. Today it is home to a multiplicity of political organisations and a diversity of houses of religious worship. Ease of access too has played its part in projecting the illusion of the promised land. From the Romans through to the Irish, Jews, Chinese, African-Caribbeans and Africans, the River Thames has facilitated the creation of 'Cosmopolitan London', whilst in the jet age London's airports are amongst the busiest in the world, dealing with the arrival, and return, of peoples from all parts of the globe.

**Patterns of migration**

Waterman tells us that, 'in terms of international migration...most people stay put'.[14] In Britain there has always been a reluctance to move from one region to another, in London an unwillingness to settle on the unfamiliar side of the Thames. However, all our contributors are agreed on the fact that, in terms of mass migration, - that is movements which create significant spatial displacement[15] - the outstanding characteristic is the chain created by voluntary and involuntary movements when the vanguard is succeeded by the masses. The Huguenots established a chain several decades before the Revocation of the Edict of Nantes in 1685, the Irish set-up patterns of seasonal migration well before the famines of the 1820s and 1840s turned seasonality into permanency. Jews, Bangladeshis, Chinese, African-Caribbeans...all had their pioneers who pinpointed the first point of settlement and laid the foundations, however precarious, for kith and kin to follow; the interval between first settlement and mass entry, as in the case of the Bangladeshis, sometimes taking years rather than months.

Godley and Waterman show us that the chain persists beyond the first stage. It is also a feature of second stage regional and social mobility. In his study of the regional mobility of eastern European Jews before the First World War, Godley challenges established theories of immigrant regional mobility, weighing up the competing influences of economic and socio-political forces. Waterman takes the mobility of the Jews one, or more, steps further and by so doing questions the geographic perception of London, a capital which has expanded into the suburbs and green belt. As the boundaries move are the concepts of the Promised Land changing too? Has the image become two dimensional, urban/suburban, with the centre still exerting its magnetic force, retaining both those who have been unable to achieve the dream and those who, as Waterman suggests, have sufficient wealth to afford to move back into the more salubrious parts of what today we know as 'central' London? Reference has been made above to the impact of the post modern economy on patterns of migration. All over the globe, glass and steel buildings herald spatial economic movement. Around London's newest boundary, the M25, new business centres abound, the city extended out to previously independent towns such as Southend-on-Sea, Watford and Harlow.

Fenton suggests that in certain instances the pattern of assimilation and settlement is changing, and that not all migrants will want, or need, to undertake the second stage. He refers to the way in which Bangladeshis in the Bethnal Green City Challenge area of Tower Hamlets 'have a lesser desire to move out than other groups', and find it 'quite a good place to live'. Improvements in housing conditions, diversified business opportunities and improving standards of academic achievement may well result in a changed perception of the first point of settlement, even so, one can only conjecture as to whether the first point of settlement could ever become the promised land.[16]

At this stage it is impossible to refer to a final stage in the history of patterns of migration. Whilst for the Jews from eastern Europe and the famine stricken Irish in the nineteenth century, return was rarely on the agenda,[17] today, the eventual goal is far from clear. Where is the final place of settlement? For those migrants who came from a country which was that of their ancestors, return with riches would seem the ideal. Indeed, Nanton describes how those who return to the Caribbean are perceived as either wealthy or mad. But he provides another facet in the mosaic of migration, one born of a welfare state. Increasing numbers of African-Caribbeans are being tied to London by the social services - is the promised land where benefits are paid? Bangladeshi elders have returned home only to find they no longer fit into the rural society from which they came, they are re-migrating to London and, as their lives draw to a close, encounter a confusion in identity. (Problems of identity are being confronted by a number of immigrants, who in some cases are forced to construct a new identity as a result of contemporary religious and political pressures.[18]) Young Bangladeshis see life very differently. Whilst Fenton's findings have suggested a high percentage of satisfaction with London, Eade's survey has shown that the young people, females particularly, see themselves as part of a global society and the promised land as an abstract rather than a reality. Waterman's findings provide further food for thought. London now is home to some 16,000 Israelis; for them the promised land has made the most radical move of all.

## Conclusion

Without ambition and a desire to improve quality of life, man and woman would stay put. Reality has shown us that whilst these characteristics may be innate they are activated at different levels and at different times, thus producing variations in the density and chronology of the movements of people. Whilst it is obvious that certain features of the migrant experience have changed over the centuries, we still need to evaluate how, and if, the concept and experience has altered. Groups and individuals have different sets of values; what might appear as riches beyond the dreams of avarice to one might be insufficient to the other; what might appear as freedom for the apolitical might be unacceptable to the political activist and radical; the ideal climate for some might be too hot, too cold or too temperate for others; the dream has its variants as does the geographic location of the promised land. Thus we have to exercise care when drawing conclusions as to levels of achievement of specific immigrant groups. Kershen illustrates that not every Huguenot and Jew 'made it' and that the assessment of Bangladeshi success has to be made on an international, not local, scale. Space must also be given to immigrant reception; xenophobia, anti-alienism and racism (Fishman describes below how the Irish and the Jews united in order to face the enemy, fascism) have all featured in the London experience and sadly continue to play their part today. These negative responses cannot be separated from contemporary economic and social conditions and one asks how much these have coloured the image of the promised land and how powerful a role they have played in subsequent migrant mobility. We need to assess not only how the concept of the promised land has changed over the centuries but, in addition, whether a change takes place during an individual's lifetime and, if so, why and how. We need to look at the issue of role model's to see whether the immigrant sets his or her sights on an individual or a concept; on the soccer star, entrepreneur, property owner, lawyer, accountant or simply 'success' and 'power'. The assimilation and acculturation processes require analysis in order to assess the immigrant experience in terms of education, culture, language and socio-economic mobility.

The main question posed in this volume is whether London has been the promised land for those who have sought economic opportunity, political and religious freedom and refuge within its boundaries. In addition we ask; was the perception of the promised land born out by the reality, or has London let its immigrants down; has the history of settlement in the capital been one of isolation or of interaction with both native and other ethnic groups; has the pattern been to stay put or to move on, not only from the first point of settlement but regionally and internationally? Finally, what of the future, will London continue to see successive waves of migrants settling in the traditional areas or will current immigration controls succeed in keeping out the 'strangers' that in previous times added their culture, religion and labour to the capital's kaleidoscope? It is a question to be addressed, though far too early to proffer an answer.[19]

**Notes**

---

[1] *New Holy Bible*, Exodus, Ch. III, Verse 10.

[2] See M. Marrus, *The Unwanted*, Oxford, Oxford University Press, 1995, Ch. 1.

[3] See L. Gartner, *The Jewish Immigrant in England 1870-1914*, London, George Allen & Unwin, 1960, Chs. 1, 2. See Marrus, op. cit.

[4] R. Cohen, *Cambridge Dictionary of Migration*, Cambridge, Cambridge University Press, 1995, p. 2.

[5] For a survey of indentured labour on a global level see A. Segal, *Atlas of International Migration*, London, Hans Zell, 1993.

[6] See Ch. 5 below.

[7] J. Johnson and J. Salt (editors), *Labour Migration*, London, David Fulton, 1990, p. 1.

[8] See A. Sherman, *Island Refuge*, London, Paul Elek, 1973 and M. Berghahn, *Continental Britons. German-Jewish Refugees from Nazi Germany*, Leamington Spa, Berg, 1988 and Holmes, Ch. 2 below.

[9] On 3 November 1996, BBC2's programme *Assignment* investigated current European immigration policies and the ways by which illegal entrants are finding more and more convoluted methods of entry into Europe.

[10] See Ch. 2.

[11] See C. Holmes, *A Tolerant Country?*, London, Faber and Faber, 1991.

[12] See A.J. Kershen, *Uniting the Tailors*, London, Frank Cass, 1995, Ch. 2.

[13] M. Seller, *To Seek America*, New Jersey, Ozer, 1988, p. 197.

[14] See below Ch. 9.

[15] See R. King (editor), *Mass Migration In Europe*, London, Belhaven Press, 1993.

[16] In some instances Bethnal Green is the second point of settlement, the Bangladeshis having moved out of the poor and overcrowded housing that characterised Spitalfields in the 1970s and early 1980s into improved housing in Bethnal Green. See C. Foreman, *Spitalfields: A Battle for Land*, London, Hilary Shipman, 1989.

[17] A small percentage of eastern European Jews returned to Russia and Russia Poland at the end of the 19th Century as a result of their failure in the west, inability to withstand the harsh and exploitative conditions, a need for family or, in very few cases, to enjoy the proceeds of the sojourn. For further details see M. Marrus, op. cit., p. 32.

[18] The next volume to be published by the Centre for the Study of Migration, late 1988, will be entitled *A Question of Identity* and will deal with the problem in a global context.

[19] It is impossible in a volume of this nature and size to examine all the various immigrant groups that have settled in the capital city. Colin Holmes provides us with an overview but in the main the groups examined are the Irish, Jews, Huguenots, Bangladeshis and African Caribbeans. For a brief outline of the different immigrant groups who have settled in London over the centuries see N. Merriman (editor), *The Peopling of London*, London, Museum of London, 1993.

# 2 Cosmopolitan London

*Colin Holmes*

In the 1880 edition of his book, *The Huguenots*, Samuel Smiles, the apostle of self-help, wrote of London as 'the world's asylum...the refuge of the persecuted of all lands...[and] probably one of the most composite populations to be found in the world.'[1] Later, at the turn of the century, the role of the capital in the country's immigration history becomes clear from a reading of George Sims' edited volumes on *Living London*.[2] This image is also captured in the book which accompanied the successful recent exhibition, mounted by the Museum of London, on overseas settlement in the capital.[3]

Yet, important as it is within the history of the national picture, no attempt has yet been made to pull together the various existing strands and many loose ends of the history of immigration into London. Attention needs to be drawn not only to immigrants who left their native countries for a variety of economic, social, or cultural reasons - often for a mixture of such influences - but also to refugees who sought shelter on account of a real or perceived threat of racial, religious or political persecution.

## The mosaic of immigration

In considering the historical panorama of immigration into London the wealth of evidence alone demands a degree of chronological restraint. The Lombards and the Jews of the medieval epoch, the Hansa merchants, and the Huguenots of the early modern period, as well as the procession of refugees of a later vintage, including the arrivals from France after 1789 and the multitude of nationalities who came after the 1848 Revolutions, all left their various marks in the capital. Houses built by the Huguenots in the area around Spital Square and Fournier Street, still stand. And, from later years, Giuseppe Panizzi's blue-domed reading room in the British Museum, the 'home' of many later refugees, is one marvellous legacy of the mid-nineteenth century immigration from Europe.

However, my focus here is upon primary immigration from the late nineteenth century onwards, starting at a time when London's population exceeded that of every other city in the world. The early years of this period witnessed the arrival of people, mainly Jews, who came from Russian Poland.[4] There is no precise figure on the number of Jews who arrived in Britain from the Tsar's Empire, from which they were driven westwards by economic pressures and persecution. However, it is apparent that London, along with Leeds and Manchester, became one of the major areas of settlement in England. Within the capital the majority of newcomers settled within the East End and, inside that area of the city, their major concentration occurred in Stepney. In 1901 an estimated 80 per cent of the 53,537 Russian Poles in London lived in that quarter and, at the time of the census return of that year, 63 per cent of the Russian Poles in England and Wales could be found in London. Not that these foreigners, even when added to the other people of alien nationality in London, constituted a large percentage of the people living in the capital: at the time of the 1901 return foreigners accounted for only 30 out of every 1,000 of London's population.[5] But to return to the Russian Poles. The level of their immigration in the late nineteenth century was such that by 1901 they constituted the largest single minority from continental Europe then living in England and Wales, a position which, until the 1890s had been occupied by the Germans, whose presence reflected various economic, social, or political pressures in Germany as well as the pull of circumstances in Britain, an interactive process which, in common with other contemporary migrations, was smoothed by the improvement in communications.[6]

These Germans, like the Russian Poles, had become heavily concentrated in London. According to the 1901 Census, 27,427 out of a total German population of 49,133 in England and Wales, lived in London. That concentration had been apparent for some time. Hence the observation: 'The most striking point [about the Germans] is that throughout the Victorian and Edwardian periods about half the German population of England and Wales lived in London.'[7] The small section of St Pancras, bordered by Tottenham Court Road, Mortimer Street, Cleveland Street and Euston Road, had become marked by the early twentieth century as a particularly important German enclave.

The Germans were manoeuvred into an uncomfortable position as Britain and Germany drifted towards the outbreak of war. Once hostilities commenced, a further deterioration ensued and the deportation of enemy aliens by the British Government effectively broke the back of the German community.[8] It was not until the 1930s and the arrival between 1933 and 1939 of 56,000 refugees from the Greater Germany, consisting particularly of Jews in flight from Nazism, that the German-born community in Britain became more evident. As with the earlier newcomers from Germany, some of whom had also been Jewish, London acted as a magnet for the refugees of the 1930s.[9] Not that they revealed any great interest in beating a path towards the East End where the Russian Polish Jews had concentrated a few years before: these Central Europeans (people born in Austria and Czechoslovakia added to the numbers from Germany) directed themselves essentially towards North London. It is in this part of the capital that the curious can peer at Sigmund Freud's consulting couch at 20 Maresfield Gardens, NW3.

Soon afterwards, the world conflict of 1939 to 1945 drew a cosmopolitan collection of military personnel into Britain, including troops from the Commonwealth and the United States. But Europeans also came. London provided a base in exile for Czech, French and Polish groups, among others, some of whom stayed after the war.[10] Furthermore, following the hostilities London served as a magnet for the Irish, whose immigration reached particularly high levels. At the beginning of the century 60,211 Irish were counted in London in the 1901 Census and another 33,850 were recorded in the adjoining counties of Surrey, Kent, Middlesex, and Sussex. This figure exceeded the size of any European group at this time and constituted a good proportion of the 426,565 Irish recorded as present in that census in England and Wales. On moving ahead ninety years, the Irish from the Republic still constituted the largest single immigrant minority in Britain. In addition, these Irish constituted the largest ethnic group by immigration to London, where the population of the Irish born in the Republic totalled 214,083.[11] Economic and cultural pressures had long worked to encourage emigration from Ireland but the upsurge in the entry of the Irish after 1945 owed a good deal to the opportunities for work in the re-building of Britain and, later, the appeal of the cultural ambience of the 1960s for many young Irish people.

However, in these post-war years, in common with the rest of Britain, the attention directed towards immigrants in London shifted primarily onto those groups who arrived from beyond Europe. Blacks and Asians, from 'beyond the oceans' had long been present in Britain and numbers had grown during the Second World War. In the course of the hostilities labour from the Empire, in the shape of merchant seamen, for example, as well as military personnel, had increased the size of Black and Asian groups.[12] However, after 1945 people from the Caribbean and the Indian sub-continent arrived in greater numbers than ever before. Deep historical links have been forged between Britain and the Caribbean, as well as with the Indian sub-continent and this Imperial connection was reflected in the long-standing contact through immigration. But after 1945 a primary, though not sole, pressure which influenced immigration from these areas was the opportunity to gain employment at relatively high levels of pay, at a time of labour shortage. Hence the close correlation between immigration and movements in the economy. Another group from Asia, the ethnic Chinese, also grew substantially in number and Chinese settlements, especially in London and Manchester, jumped appreciably in size, albeit from a low base.[13] A long tradition of emigration exists among the Chinese and against this background Hong Kong provided the base for much of this post-war immigration. Economic pressures in the colony, as well as political uncertainty, helped to fuel the exit of ethnic Chinese, particularly up to 1971. The shrinking of the world through the improvement in communications also facilitated this process, as it did other migrations. The Hong Kong Chinese were also aware of economic opportunities, particularly the niche in the restaurant sector. In considering the link of such migrations to London, it is clear that in the 1990s, the area of Greater London is the chief centre of settlement in Britain for such Black and Asian immigrant groups and their descendants.[14]

In brief, London has witnessed a regular contact with the process of immigration into Britain. At times, indeed, it has assumed a critical significance in the settlement of certain immigrants and refugee minorities. For some individuals drawn from such groups their only experience of Britain has been bounded by the geographical expanse of the capital.

Against this background there is no intention to mount a comprehensive coverage of immigration into London, a task which, even if focused on the years from the late nineteenth century onwards, can be accomplished, arguably, only by a team of researchers drawn from different disciplines. The aim is more modest: it is to ask: why did such immigrants and refugees settle in London? How were they received? How did they influence the capital's development?

## London the magnet

The question arises first: why London? Why did immigrants and refugees concentrate there? The function of the city as a port provides part of the explanation. Refugees escaping from the revolutions, or counter revolutions, in nineteenth or early twentieth century Europe often had their first glimpse of Britain when they sailed up the Thames. Carrying with them expectations of an early return to their roots, they stayed where they first landed. Much later the docks at Tilbury witnessed the arrival in 1948 of the *Empire Windrush* with its passengers from the Caribbean who can be counted among the pioneers of post-war Black immigration. Some of these newcomers also decided to remain where they landed. There is nothing unusual or exceptional in this pattern. Liverpool remains the most Irish of English cities because it is there that many Irish immigrants first set foot in Britain and they have stayed in the city or fanned out only a short distance to the surrounding areas of Lancashire.

However, in the case of London, other influences have played their part in attracting immigrants and refugees. Between 1939 and 1945, the wartime capital buzzed with cosmopolitan voices: this much has already been noticed. Émigrés from vanquished, and in some cases vanished, nations found it convenient to locate in London because leaders of exiled groups could keep in touch with the political and bureaucratic centres of political power in Britain: hence the presence of wartime Governments-in-exile such as those representing the Czech, Polish and French interests.[15]

This importance of London as a centre of political power also helped to account for the arrival in the early twentieth century of students and other activists from Africa, the Caribbean and the Indian sub-continent. In the views of such people London functioned as 'the junction box of the Empire' where political wires could be pulled and manipulated Their aim was to secure the independence of their countries, to free themselves from British control. Not that such individuals failed to have an influence on London during their years in the capital. Krishna Menon, for example, left his mark on the borough of St. Pancras. The political leverage on issues of national independence which the individuals could exert increased during the Second World War but that influence drew heavily upon earlier contacts.[16]

For other arrivals the lure of politics exercised a lower priority. Pushed from their own countries by the pressures of economic problems, immigrants congregated in London because it offered employment. In the nineteenth century various European groups, such as the Germans and Italians, found work in London's West End in the expanding service sector. German clerks busied themselves in the counting houses of the City of London.[17] Italians helped to develop the capital's restaurants.[18] Both groups also found work in other sectors of the economy: Germans appear as sugar refiners and bakers and Italians could be heard as street musicians or were sought after for their ice cream. The immigration since 1945 of Blacks and Asians needs to be placed within the context of a general post-war movement into the sprawling conurbations that were losing population and where these immigrants could serve as a replacement labour force. For many newcomers, then, their presence in London was related to the material forces playing upon their lives, through which they formed a permanent feature of the capital's labour force.[19]

All these various movements developed a self-feeding aspect. Russian Polish Jews leaving the Tsar's domains, followed their kinsman to London. Among Italians, who arrived at the same time as these Jews, a similar process can be traced. Family ties and friendship patterns also became woven into the later immigration of Blacks and Asians. Letters sent home often provided intelligence on the prospects in London. Intending immigrants could be quite knowledgeable about the labour market in London whilst they still lived in the Caribbean or on the Indian sub-continent.

## A tolerant London?

How have these various groups been received since they came to the capital? When it suits their purpose policy makers can proclaim that Britain is a tolerant country, 'the very cradle of liberty and tolerance, the most law-abiding country in the world',[20] markedly different from other societies in its responses to immigrants and refugees. It has been emphasised already that the East End constituted one important area of settlement within London and in 1982 Ian Mikardo, who then represented the Bow and

Poplar constituency for Labour, concluded that: 'The majority of East Enders are kindly and tolerant towards those around them whoever they are and wherever they come from'. He viewed that toleration as emerging from 'a sense of solidarity among people struggling to earn a living and maintain decent standards'.[21] All is for the best, therefore, a view which was trumpeted in a recent newspaper editorial: 'we are a sovereign country', it proclaimed, 'also a rather decent country which owes nobody an apology for the treatment of black or brown people. Orwellian decency runs very deep in the British'.[22]

Rather than dwell exclusively upon the superior moral qualities within the nation, there is a need to probe deeper into specific contexts in order to understand better the situations which immigrants and refugees have faced When we do, it is possible, in the case of London, to present a less glowing and glittering picture than that which dilates on the strength of a tolerant tradition. There is an abundance of detail which can be deployed against the cosy, reassuring image of society moulded and guided by the forces of toleration.

Evidence can be accumulated on tensions between the resident population of London and newcomers well before the nineteenth century. Victor Kiernan's long general essay on 'Britons Old and New' and Dorothy George's more specific study of *London Life in the Eighteenth Century*, leave no doubts on that score.[23] But what of the years from the late nineteenth century onwards? What follows is intended merely as an indication of some of the more dramatic developments which reveal the reverse side of the coin to the claims that toleration has reigned supreme.

From the 1880s the arrival of Russian Polish Jews in London, and also in major provincial centres such as Leeds and Manchester, provided the impetus to a fierce public debate on whether or not to control alien immigration. Restrictions imposed on foreigners in 1793 had been effectively lifted by 1826. Between 1848 and 1850, at the time of revolutionary upheavals in Europe, the British Government once again assumed powers which would have enabled it to control the entry of aliens. In practice such legislation was never deployed and in subsequent years entry remained unrestricted However, the immigration from the Tsar's Empire exercised a decisive influence in changing that state of affairs.[24]

Agitation centred particularly, if not exclusively, on the East End of London, the major area of Russian Polish settlement where, at the time of this immigration, the extent of the area's economic and social problems stood starkly revealed in Charles Booth's surveys and also, in dramatic style, in Andrew Mearns' *Bitter Cry of Outcast London*, as well as even more sensationally in the Ripper murders of 1888. In East London, grassroots' opposition, stimulated by pressures in the housing and labour markets, acting in tandem with cultural conflicts, emerged as central to the debate. Moreover, with the formation in the East End of the British Brothers' League in 1901, such opposition secured a link, through the support it received from various Conservative MPs, with the decision-making process in Westminster.[25]

By 1902 the so-called alien problem was regarded in some quarters as 'the most pressing problem of east London life'[26] and in January of that year a large meeting of the British Brothers' League at the People's Palace swelled to the sounds of 'There's no place like home' and 'Soldiers of the Queen' before hearing a litany of abuse heaped upon aliens.[27] At one point in his address to the meeting A.T. Williams proclaimed:

> I don't care for statistics. God has given me a pair of eyes in my head - and as I walk through Mile End or Cable Street, as I walk about your streets, I see names have changed; I see good old names of tradesmen have gone, and in their places are foreign names - the names of those who have ousted Englishmen into the cold (at which point there were loud cries of 'Shame' and 'wipe them out').[28]

It is clear from the history of the BBL, and the surrounding forces which led to the 1905 Aliens Act, that antipathies towards alien immigration, focused especially on the Russian Poles, developed an increasingly sharper edge in the early years of the present century. The arrival of these East European Jews heightened the connection already made in the condition of England debate between urban problems and potential revolution.

Not that the 1905 Act, which laid down a process of discretionary entry for aliens, marked the end of opposition towards the Russian Poles.[29] Attitudes towards this group helped to account for the 1919 Aliens Act. This measure, parts of which remained in force until the 1971 Immigration Act, placed an even more decisive control on the entry and residence of aliens and simultaneously increased the State's powers in relation to their deportation.[30]

An attempt to account for the 1919 Act exclusively in terms of a response to Russian Polish immigration, however, would fall wide of the mark. By the time the Act entered the Statute Book, the Germans in Britain had become a major focus of hostile attention and the opposition they met as enemy aliens during the First World War contributed to the vicious anti-alien ambience in 1919. In the early days of the war, in 1914 and 1915, the Germans encountered collective violence in London and in other centres. In 1915 the level of such hostility in the capital has been described recently as 'extremely serious'.[31] Kentish Town featured in the forefront of such violence but it spread across London and on 13 May 1915 *The Times* claimed that in the East End, 'Every man seemed to have given up the day to an anti-German orgy'.[32] In the later expressions of anti-German violence, Acton, Islington and Tooting all erupted with hostility in June 1916 following the loss of *HMS Hampshire* with Lord Kitchener on board. London also witnessed a further serious spate of attacks on Germans in July 1917.[33]

In parallel with such developments, the State engaged in the internment and deportation of enemy aliens, including Germans. In view of such wartime experiences, it is hardly surprising that anti-German sentiment featured prominently in the parliamentary debates on the 1919 Aliens Bill.[34] Not that Germans alone had to contend with violence in London during the First World War. 'War's big drum' and the demand for 'live meat to be spitted on iron', to quote Mayakovsky, required absolute loyalty and in such circumstances the behaviour of friendly aliens also created tension. The history of the Russian Polish Jews in Britain between 1914 and 1918 confirms that observation. The reluctance of these Jews to engage in military service led to attacks in Leeds in June 1917. Then, in the following September, London followed suit. Clashes between Russian Jews and the local population occurred in Euston early that month. But the major disturbances came shortly afterwards in Bethnal Green on 23 and 24 September, in a series of incidents which at one stage involved a crowd of 5,000 people.[35] Some of the targets of such violence, who had escaped from a country of pogroms only a few years before, must have wondered what lay in store for them in the land that they had chosen as a refuge. From a different perspective, however, the reluctance shown by many Russian Poles to shoulder arms raised the issue of their loyalty and, ultimately, to some critics, whether their presence was desirable. That theme, sharpened in the context of the war, was also fed into the debate on the 1919 Aliens Bill.[36]

It was not only the war which generated collective violence: the aftermath of the hostilities, with its own uncertainties, also brought about conflict. In 1919 a wave of violence directed against Blacks and other racial minority groups swept across Britain, and London was not immune from such tension. A common thread in such hostility was an emphasis on reversing the economic and social gains which these minorities had secured at a time of labour scarcity during the war. The violence began in Glasgow in January 1919 and had spread to Canning Town in the May and June of that year.[37] It was following such incidents and the passing of the 1919 Aliens Act that the LCC, feeding off this ambience of xenophobia, took steps to ensure that aliens faced discrimination in the authority's provision of education, employment, and housing services.[38]

Any attempt to create a sense of distance between these unfolding events and more recent times, in order to nourish a sense of greater enlightenment with the passing of time, is calculated to break down. Evidence in support of the pessimistic tone can be marshalled quite easily. One thinks of the attacks on immigrant Jews and their children in the East End when Oswald Mosley turned the BUF towards a campaign in East London, a clash which became symbolised and mythologised by the Battle of Cable Street on 4 October 1936. Here the BUF attempted to draw upon the existing culture of anti-semitism which circulated within East London and focused on Jews as the agents of both local and national problems.[39]

Then, too, the post-war years provide further detail on the persistence of collective violence. In the bleak context of the post-war world and the beginnings of immigration from the Caribbean, hostility against Blacks became a prominent feature of inter-group relations. In 'a skirmish in London over several nights between Whites and Blacks in Deptford Broadway in July 1949...a crowd of 1000 Whites besieged a number of Blacks who were staying in a local hostel...'.[40] Then, in 1954 in Camden Town, 'black people...defended themselves against white attackers whose weapons included a petrol bomb thrown into a house occupied by a West Indian family'.[41] However, these incidents soon became overshadowed by the so-called race riots in Nottingham and Notting Hill in August 1958. This hostility had some of its roots in the housing problems of the post-war years which were exacerbated by the process of immigration. But such tensions also gained momentum, particularly in London, from the calculated and assiduous fanning of such flames by fascist groups. The upshot was violence on a considerable scale. 'By the end of August', it has been written, 'brawls, disturbances and racist attacks were a daily and nightly feature of life in north Kensington. A Jamaican was shot in the leg. Petrol bombs were thrown into black people's homes, including the homes of a pregnant women.... Crowds hundreds strong shouted abuse at black people.... Sensational press reports generated extra excitement.'[42] From these roots between 1958 and 1959 racial violence spread to other parts of London, and led to incidents in Kensal Green, Hornsey, Islington, Hackney and Stepney.[43]

This discussion of hostility began by referring to developments in East London and, by way of a final observation, it is possible to return there. The Paki-bashing incidents perpetrated by skinheads in 1971 and a number of racially motivated murders in 1978 revealed the continuity of racial violence and harassment in the capital's deprived areas. But the headlines on these and later incidents can obscure only too easily what has been described as: 'an almost continuous and unrelenting battery of Asian people and their poverty in the East End of London'.[44] Further evidence, less dramatic in character, but also significant for those who had to endure it, would have to be considered if a wider perspective were adopted. Verbal and written hostility, as well as various forms of discriminatory treatment, have all contributed to the total history of immigrants and refugees in the capital.[45]

However, it would be a distortion as seriously flawed as that which characterises Britain as uniquely tolerant, if the picture were left at this juncture. Some groups of immigrants and refugees have survived and generally prospered in Britain. In the case of London the movement of Jews from the East End to Golders Green and the surrounding districts provides some evidence on this score. The haven afforded to refugees in London as well as other cities has protected individuals and groups whether they remained permanently in exile, like many Poles after 1945, or, as in the case of some nineteenth century refugees, for a brief but decisive phase in their lives. Compared with their earlier experiences émigré life for many such groups, whatever its problems, did mark an improvement. Certainly, it should not be assumed, even bearing in mind the catalogue of hostility which can be compiled, that London was a perpetual hell-hole. Hostility was persistent, but it has to be realised that it was stronger at certain times than others and linked to specific circumstances rather than generalised: the First World War and its immediate aftermath was a particularly decisive period for it. Outside such contexts there was much ambiguity and ambivalence in public responses. But after conceding these points and also recognising that other major cities such as Berlin and New York have witnessed similar tensions since the nineteenth century, the opposition which surfaced in London should not remain a blank spot, repressed or qualified, in order to foster a brighter image. In the challenging words of Hannah Arendt, delivered in a different context: 'We can no longer afford to take that which was good in the past and call it our heritage, to discard the bad and simply to think of it as a dead load which by itself time will bury in oblivion.'[46]

**Contributions to London**

However, there is another dimension to set alongside these so-far predominant dark hues. That other aspect requires a recognition of the varied economic and cultural contributions which immigrants and refugees have made to the capital's history. Evidence on this theme can be accumulated long before the late nineteenth century. But if the focus remains on the last hundred years or so, a beginning can be made by reminding ourselves initially of economic activities. The role of immigrants in the history of the City is undoubtedly significant and, specifically, the influence of Germans and German Jews is quite striking. The names of Cassel, Speyer, and Schroeder, are inseparable from the City's progress before 1914 to international pre-eminence in the world of finance. Outsiders refreshed and stimulated such activity, not only in Britain but also in other countries. In the words of one observer: 'There is no doubt at all that in the thirty years or so before World War I Jewish houses were conspicuously active in the major financial centres.'[47]

Since then the entrepreneurial energy expended by immigrants and refugees has continued to influence London's economy. After 1945 one thinks of immigrant businessmen in the service sector, particularly, for example in the food business; Chinese restaurateurs, as well as their Cypriot and Italian equivalents, represent part of a wider sample. It is difficult to imagine London without thinking of their enterprises. In recent times, Soho, a traditional cosmopolitan area of the capital, has perhaps provided the most noticeable concentration of such activity but ethnic restaurants are a feature of virtually every part of London.[48]

Nevertheless, there are dangers in concentrating exclusively on such entrepreneurial activity. Immigrant and refugee groups are seldom homogeneous. They contain individuals who are separated by class and status, as well as other differences. Consequently, a variety of inputs should be expected from their presence. With this awareness, it is instructive also to consider the contributions of labour. In the late nineteenth and early twentieth centuries when German financiers were enjoying their success and moving up the social scale, the German clerks employed in merchant banking were utilising their skill at language, encouraged by the German educational system, to build the businesses of their employers and bring London into closer contact with the developing commercial and financial centres of Europe.[49]

But labour's contributions proved more extensive. The Black and Asian seamen who helped to man the ships which entered the port of London, and whose settlements could be found in the East End, performed a service which helped the capital to function. Their ships carried essential cargoes. Such goods would often be unloaded by Irish dockers. Some of the cargoes would be consumed in the West End's houses and hotels, a number of which would have been built with the assistance of Irish construction workers. In such hotels it was likely that guests would be catered for by continental Europeans, particularly from France, Germany and Italy, whose labour constituted a recognisable element in the service sector.

The varied contributions of labour did not cease as the twentieth century wore on. The Irish who had assisted in the building of the capital infrastructure in the nineteenth century, continued with their involvement in the civil engineering industry, working, as the song reminds us, for firms such as McAlpine, Wimpey and John Laing. If the social structure of the Irish minority became more diverse after 1945, with a greater presence of professional people, even so, an Irish link with 'the buildings' remained significant. Irish labour helped to build the Festival of Britain site and, more recently, it has been employed in fair numbers by Olympia and York on the construction of the new ziggurat penetrating the sky at Canary Wharf.[50] Immigrant labour, particularly of Blacks and Asians, has also provided a recognisable element in the public sector workforce of London, whether in hospitals or on London Transport.[51]

During the major period of primary immigration in the post-war years, essentially up to 1971, immigrant labour performed other tasks. Black seamen remained important in the merchant navy in the early post-war years and congregated in areas such as Stepney. The tailoring trade also depended heavily on male and female immigrants. Whereas in the late nineteenth century Jewish immigrant workers had reinforced the sweating system, in the post-war years the workforce was more likely to be, say, Bangladeshi or Turkish Cypriot. In addition, labour from the Indian sub-continent threw an economic lifeline in the 1950s and 1960s to certain firms in Southall which had found it difficult to recruit workers. In many cases the conditions in these industries, and also in other areas of employment, left much to be desired. But such workers had to contend with more than problems in their workplace. They often lived in rundown areas of the capital where they inhabited inferior housing and in their daily tasks they frequently encountered antipathy and discrimination. As such, their life histories were not the easy stuff of headlines committed to emphasise success and improvement. But these often silent and largely invisible men and women ought not to be forgotten.[52]

Getting and spending we lay waste our powers, so the good book tells us, but in identifying the consequences which have followed from immigration, the historian needs to transcend economic categories. Various cultural outcomes also call for attention. Some of the immigrants and refugees who came to Britain were intellectuals. Scholars could certainly be counted amongst the Communard refugees.[53] But perhaps the most striking case of an influx of refugee scholars arose with the immigration in the early twentieth century from Central and Eastern Europe and particularly from the Greater Germany in the 1930s.[54] The collective expertise of refugees among these groups spread across a wide span of disciplines and a number of scholars have left their imprint on the cultural landscape. 'Their quality and originality [varied] greatly but their collective role [was] indisputable.'[55]

A number of these émigrés are associated particularly with London: Ernst Gombrich, later Director of the Warburg Institute, Karl Popper, philosopher and Karl Mannheim, sociologist. Both Popper and Mannheim, as well as the social anthropologist, Ernest Gellner, pursued careers which were linked to the history of the LSE. Indeed, when the history of that institution is discussed, it becomes impossible to ignore the influence of émigrés. Some time after those already named, Imre Lakatos arrived following the Hungarian Revolution of 1956, and quickly made his mark on the philosophy of science.[56]

Intellectual life is not confined to universities and, on stepping outside the academy, there is no difficulty in finding numerous instances of work which derived from artists and scholars who had immigrated to London. Some of these cultural artefacts have remained marginalized. The poetry of the Yiddish writers, Stencl and Morris Winchevsky,[57] and, later, the art of the Guyanese painter, Aubrey Williams, who also based himself in the capital, have achieved very limited degrees of recognition.[58] The output of some other writers and artists occupies more of a 'limbo' position. Samuel Selvon's, *The Lonely Londoners* is the definitive novel of immigrant West Indian life in London in the 1950s, but does it yet swim in the mainstream of English literature?[59] And does George Mikes' *How To Be An Alien*, a

Hungarian perspective on life in exile, count for more than a humorous curiosity?[60] In other cases, by contrast, a greater degree of salience has been achieved. The sculpture of Jacob Epstein, who worked in London from 1905, provides one controversial example.[61] So does the work of Feliks Topolski, an exile from Poland who became, 'very much a South Bank man and proud of being an adopted Londoner'. It was this Topolski who produced the Cavalcade of the Commonwealth for the 1951 Festival of Britain.[62] One can also recall in this gallery, Victor Weisz, 'Vicky', the Hungarian cartoonist, who came to Britain from Berlin and made London and its newspaper world on Fleet Street his new base.[63] It is likely that all these individuals, as well as others such as Bill Brandt and Wolf Suschitzky, two visual artists who caught the atmosphere of twentieth-century London in their creative activity, would have produced important works even if they had not migrated from their birthplaces. But move they did, and it was in London that finally they settled and worked. Whether or not their creativity was enhanced by the tensions, both positive and negative, associated with their movement remains an elusive question.

Let us leave individual achievement and move back to general observations, noticing firstly the influence of immigration on the capital's religious life. In London, as in other cities in Britain, the Irish since the nineteenth century greatly assisted the growth of Roman Catholicism, even if the relationship between the Irish and the Church was not without its ambivalence. The offerings of the Irish poor contributed to the building of churches, Irish people also added to the size of the Roman Catholic congregations, and priests from Ireland laboured across the water.[64] But the religious impact derived from immigration has transcended the history of Christianity in London. The building at the end of Fournier Street in Spitalfields began life as a Huguenot Church in 1744; it served as an Orthodox Synagogue at the time of the immigration from Russian Poland; today it is a mosque. That one building provides vivid testimony to some of the different religious cultures which have become woven into the capital's history.[65] The mosque in Regents Park, the Gujerati temple in Neasden, and Greek Orthodox places of worship, such as the Church of All Saints in Camden Town, are further signs of the diversity of religious life which immigration has introduced into Britain, changing the cultural map of London in the process.

It is not only the sacred dimension of cultural transference which stands out. There is also a less visible secular component. The political refugees who entered London in the course of the nineteenth century consisted of individuals and groups of varying persuasions. Some, like that arch-conservative Count Metternich, scurried home as soon as possible, in his case to the Austrian Empire. However, Marx, who arrived in 1849, lived at various London addresses and worked in the British Museum, endured a permanent exile. It was from London that he, along with other German exiles, helped to influence the development of Socialism, not only in Britain but internationally.[66] Just after Marx's death in 1883 - he lies buried in Highgate - the course of Socialism in Britain was further advanced by those Russian Polish Jews, heavily concentrated in London, some of whom had joined the Socialist ranks in Russia and then proceeded to bring their ideology with them on their westward migration. The cause of Anarchism was also boosted by a Russian, Polish, and also a German, presence. A little later, the foundation of a Communist Party of Great Britain in 1920 owed not little to the activities and commitment of Socialists among London's Jews: this inter-relationship was indeed to continue and mature in the course of the early twentieth century.[67]

## Discovering cosmopolitan London

The time has come to conclude. Anyone who walks through London soon catches signs of the immigrations which have become merged into its history. A study of the blue plaques studded on properties can be instructive, testifying as they do to the presence of individual immigrants and refugees. Certain houses such as that in north London designed by Ernö Goldfinger and reflecting the modern movement, are linked to the process of immigration and some of its implications. So are memorials, including the plaque at St. Peter's Church in Clerkenwell remembering the Italians who died in the *Arandora Star* tragedy.[68] Some areas also provide strong evidence of immigration. Stockwell Road in South London says Portuguese. In Spitalfields one encounters a mix of cultures. Green Lane in north London, running from Newington Green to Haringey, is of central significance to many Greek and Turkish Cypriots. Ealing has been an important area of settlement for Poles since after the end of the Second World War. Moreover, specific events testify to London's importance as a centre of immigration. The Notting Hill Carnival, the marking of St. Patrick's Day, and the procession of Our Lady of Mount Carmel, which has been held in mid-July since 1883 in Clerkenwell and Holborn, are among the reminders of immigration into London.[69]

In considering the movement into the capital which such symbols represent, continuities and differences become evident. Throughout the nineteenth and twentieth centuries London has functioned as a magnet attracting both immigrants and refugees. However, in the very recent past a noticeable increase has occurred in the size of those groups which have arrived from beyond Europe, albeit within a general context in which immigration has still consisted primarily of European groups.

Changes in spatial concentrations are also apparent. The East End, a traditional immigration reservoir, to use Beatrice Webb's imagery, has remained an important place of settlement, even though the groups walking along its streets have changed Jews can still be found in Brick Lane. But there is now a much more noticeable Asian presence, particularly of Bangladeshis.[70] There are also other significant shifts in settlement. The Irish, although highly mobile within London in the nineteenth century, did have a recognisable presence along the banks of the river where they remained close to the docks: in the course of the present century, however, they have settled in areas such as Kilburn. Pennyfields, the haunt of 'Chinatown Annie', no longer provides the central point of Chinese life in London: that role has passed in the course of the twentieth century to the West End, in particular Gerrard Street.[71] Finally, in the late nineteenth century one would have been hard pressed to find any Blacks and Asians in Brixton. At that time the district remained the preserve of music hall *artistes* and white collar workers. The Black presence, now a feature of that area of London, is a more recent phenomenon, associated with London's post-war history.[72]

In concentrating upon the history of primary immigration into the capital since the nineteenth century the spotlight has been directed partly towards the reception awarded to the immigrants and refugees. That enquiry has revealed that their immigration and settlement did not always proceed smoothly. On the contrary, the various strands of antipathy and prejudice, evident at the level of ideas, together with acts of discrimination, as well as episodes of collective violence, reveal significant lapses from that carefully crafted and well-preserved image of Britain as a uniquely tolerant country. The evidence which qualifies that image cannot be washed away by diverting attention to the torrent of greater abuses in other countries and urban centres, although to re-emphasise, the history of immigrants and refugees in London, even in the East End where much hostility can be traced, was not characterised by continual, universal opposition. Ambivalence, ambiguity, and support for such groups, can also be traced.[73] At all times the formation and direction of such responses were significantly influenced by local and national contexts.[74]

The other major theme commanding attention has grown out of the need to recognise that newcomers have helped to influence the development of Britain. Only recently has a more pronounced attempt been made to write this particular history and, in the process, to overcome the continued marginalization of the lives of immigrants and refugees.[75] In any consideration of their role in developing or creating various components of national life, a compelling need exists to unearth what has happened in London, even if there is a strong case for examining the histories of immigrants and refugees in other cities, including Bradford, Liverpool, and Manchester.[76]

One writer of alien nationality who was familiar with the capital once remarked that, 'London is so great and so complex a phenomenon and it is moreover so constantly changing, there is no reason why people should ever cease writing about it'.[77] However, to return to one of the opening emphases, much still remains to be done on the history of immigration into London, on the movement to the city where, in legend, the streets were paved with gold and ambitions could be realised In the case of those people who came to London from other countries, it serves no purpose to observe that the capital has 'a ceaseless history of immigration', if one then fails to build that awareness into accounts of London's development.[78] On a more positive note, *The Peopling of London* did attempt to make a start on that task. Indeed, it brought into its sights the history of groups such as the Americans, Somalis, Spanish, and Vietnamese, on whom it has not been possible to dwell in this present survey.[79] We need now to engage in further excavations, unearthing more evidence on what have been vital forces in London's history. There is a challenge here, which ought to be met, and soon.[80]

**Notes**

[1] S. Smiles, *The Huguenots*, London, John Murray, 1880 edition, p. 99.

---

2 G. Sims (editor), *Living London*, 3 vols., London, Cassell & Co., 1901-3.

3 N. Merriman (editor), *The Peopling of London*, London, Museum of London, 1993.

4 L. Gartner, *The Jewish Immigrant in England 1870-1914*, London, George Allen & Unwin, 1960, draws in large part on detail from London.

5 *Census of England and Wales 1901*, *Summary Tables*, London, 1903, p. 260. *Census of England and Wales 1901. General Report*, London, 1910, p. 140, and *Royal Commission on Alien Immigration*, BPP IX, 1903, p. 14, provide general and specific detail.

6 *Census 1901*, *Summary Tables*, p. 260.

7 P. Panayi, *The Enemy in Our Midst*, Oxford, Berg, 1991, pp. 16-7.

8 Ibid.

9 J.J. Barnes and P.P. Barnes, 'London's German Community in the Early 1930s', in Panayi, *Germans in Britain*, pp. 131-46 discusses the German community before the arrival of refugees from Nazism and draws its detail from London. On the refugees see M. Berghahn, *Continental Britons. German-Jewish Refugees from Nazi Germany*, Leamington Spa, Berg, 1988. For one personal testimony see G. Clare, *Last Waltz in Vienna*, London, Pan Books, 1982. For the general history and particularly on official responses see A.J. Sherman, *Island Refuge: Britain and Refugees from the Third Reich 1933-1939*, London, Paul Elek, 1973 and L. London, 'British Government Policy and Jewish Refugees 1933-1945', *Patterns of Prejudice*, Vol. 23, 1989, pp. 26-42, based on her London University Ph.D. thesis.

10 C. Holmes, *John Bull's Island. Immigration and British Society 1871-1971*, London, Macmillan, 1988, chapter IV. For a colourful account of such cosmopolitanism see W. Sansom, *Westminster at War*, London, Faber and Faber, 1947 and for an autobiographical reminiscence, see E. Raczynski, *In Allied London*, London, Weidenfeld and Nicolson, 1962.

11 University of Warwick, Centre for Research in Ethnic Relations, National Ethnic Minority Data Archive, 1991 Census Statistical Paper No. 5, *Country of Birth: Settlement Patterns*, Coventry, 1993, p. 4; *1991 Census. Greater London County Report Part 1*, London, 1993, p. 69.

12 The phrase 'beyond the oceans', is from V.G. Kiernan, 'Britons, Old and New', in C. Holmes (editor), *Immigration and British Society*, London, George Allen & Unwin, 1978, p. 54. On the history of the Blacks in Britain see P. Fryer, *Staying Power: The History of Black People in*

*Britain*, London, Pluto, 1984 and on Asians see R. Visram, *Ayahs, Lascars and Princes*, London, Pluto, 1986. On Blacks in London see P. Fraser, 'Africans and Caribbeans in London', in Merriman, op. cit., p. 51-61 and on Asians see R. Visram, 'South Asians in London', in Ibid., pp. 169-78. There is also a useful photo-history, Greater London Council, *A History of the Black Presence in London*, London, GLC, 1986.

[13] On the Chinese in Britain see D. Jones, 'The Chinese in Britain: Origins and Development of a Community', *New Community*. Vol. 7, 1979, pp. 397-402. On their London history see A. Chang, 'The Chinese in London', in Merriman, op. cit., pp. 88-97.

[14] University of Warwick, op. cit., p. 7. For a popular survey which includes detail on Blacks, Asians (from the Indian sub-continent), and ethnic Chinese, as well as Cypriots see S. Humphries and J. Taylor, *The Making of Modern London 1945-1985*, London, Sidgwick & Jackson, 1986, chapter 5.

[15] Holmes, *John Bull's Island*, Ch. IV.

[16] Specific aspects of Black political activity have been discussed recently by Duffield, Robinson, and Macdonald in J. Gundara and I. Duffield (editors), *Essays on the History of Blacks in Britain*, Aldershot, Avebury, 1992. The most accessible summary of Black and Asian activities is Fryer, op. cit., pp. 321-55.

[17] G. Anderson, *Victorian Clerks*, Manchester, Manchester University Press, 1976 and P. Panayi, *German Immigrants in Britain During the Nineteenth Century 1815-1914*, Oxford, Berg, 1995, pp. 133-4 and 266-227, for example.

[18] L. Sponza, *Italian Immigrants in Nineteenth Century Britain. Realities and Images*, Leicester, Leicester University Press, 1988.

[19] Runnymede Trust and the Radical Statistics Race Group, *Britain's Black Population*, London, Runnymede Trust, 1980, pp. 5, 7, 58 and more generally, P.G. Hall, *The Industries of London since 1861*, London, Hutchinson, 1962, p. 118.

[20] *Parliamentary Debates, Commons*, Vol. 594, 1958-9, col. 418.

[21] *Sunday Telegraph Magazine*, 11 April 1982.

[22] *Sunday Telegraph*, 3 August 1986.

[23] Kiernan, op. cit.; D. George, *London Life in the Eighteenth Century*, Oxford, Penguin, 1966 edn., Ch. 3, particularly.

[24] V. Bevan, *The Development of British Immigration Law*, London, Croom Helm, 1986, is the soundest of sources on such detail.

[25] For an evocative study of the East End at the time of the immigration which emphasises the social problems of the area, see W.J. Fishman, *East End 1888*, London, Duckworth, 1988. The BBL is discussed in C. Holmes, *Anti-Semitism in British Society 1876-1939*, London, Edward Arnold, 1978, chapter 6.

[26] *East London Advertiser*, 14 January 1902.

[27] *East London Observer*, 18 January 1902.

[28] Ibid.

[29] The impact on asylum is recognised and emphasised in B. Porter, *The Refugee Question in Mid-Victorian Politics*, Cambridge, Cambridge University Press, 1979, p. 218. On the wider context which encouraged restriction, see D. Feldman, 'The Importance of Being English. Jewish Immigration and the Decay of Liberal England' in D. Feldman and G.S. Jones (editors), *Metropolis: London Histories and Representations since 1800*, London, Routledge, 1989, pp. 56-84.

[30] D. Cesarani, 'Anti-Alienism in Britain after the First World War', *Immigrants and Minorities*, Vol. 6, 1987, pp. 15-6.

[31] Panayi, op. cit., p. 243.

[32] *The Times*, 13 May 1915.

[33] Panayi, *The Enemy in Our Midst*, pp. 253-4.

[34] See *Parliamentary Debates*, *Commons*, Vol. 168, 1919, col. 2700 and Ibid., Vol. 120, 1919, col. 1355.

[35] Holmes, *Anti-Semitism*, pp. 135-6.

[36] See generally, A.D. Smith, 'War and Ethnicity: The Role of Warfare in the Formation of Self-Images and Cohesion of Ethnic Communities', *Ethnic and Racial Studies*, Vol. 4, 1981, pp. 375-97. See Holmes, *Anti-Semitism*, Chapter 8 on the conscription issue. On the Russian Polish Jewish dimension and anti-Semitism generally, see D. Saunders, 'Aliens in Britain and the Empire During the First World War', in F. Swyripa and J.H. Thompson (editors), *Loyalties in Conflict: Ukrainians in Canada during the Great War*, Edmonton, Canadian Institute of Ukrainian Studies, University of Alberta, 1983, p. 108; *Parliamentary Debates*, *Commons*, Vol. 115, 1919, cols. 308-9 and Ibid., Vol. 120, 1919, col. 86. On the specific East End context, see J. Bush, *Behind the Lines: East London Labour 1914-1919*, London, Merlin, 1984.

[37] J. Jenkinson, 'The 1919 Riots', in P. Panayi (editor), *Racial Violence in Britain 1840-1950*, Leicester, Leicester University Press, 1993, Ch. 5.
[38] Cesarani, op. cit., p. 15.
[39] See among other sources on Cable Street, Bill Fishman's account, 'A People's Journeé: the Battle of Cable Street' in F. Krantz (editor), *History From Below: Studies in Popular Protest and Popular Ideology in Honour of George Rudé*, Montreal, Concordia University, 1985, pp. 381-94. A conference to mark the 60th anniversary of Cable Street was held at the Wiener Library on 13 October 1996. Visual evidence is available on the Yesterday's Witness programme 'The Battle for Cable Street', BBC TV, 2 January 1970. On the BUF's drive into East London, see Holmes, *Anti-Semitism*, Chs. 11 and 12. For conditions in East London see H.L. Smith (editor), *The New Survey of London Life and Labour Vol. III Survey of Social Conditions (1) The Eastern Area*, London, P.S. King, 1932.
[40] Holmes, *John Bull's Island*, p. 256.
[41] Fryer, op. cit., p. 378.
[42] Ibid., p. 379. See also E. Pilkington, *Beyond the Mother Country: West Indians and the Notting Hill White Riots*, London, I.B. Tauris, 1988.
[43] Fryer, op. cit., p. 380.
[44] Bethnal Green and Stepney Trades Council, *Blood on the Streets*, London, 1978, p. 3.
[45] Hence, for example, Joseph Banister, *England under the Jews*, London, privately printed, 1907, the most vicious expression of anti-semitism and anti-alienism, written by a London journalist, and drawing many of its arguments from their presence in the capital. Note also the violent verbal attacks by 'Mick' Clarke on East End Jews, cited in Holmes, *Anti-Semitism*, p. 183. On discrimination one might reflect on the problems which faced students, as one aspect of a wider problem. See generally A.T. Carey, 'London Landladies and Coloured Students', *Fortnightly Review*, Vol. 180, 1953, pp. 235-42. One might also recall the famous case in 1943 of racial discrimination by the Imperial Hotel against the cricketer, Learie Constantine. See Fryer, op. cit., pp. 364-6. And, as regards collective violence, one is reminded, among other instances, of the anti-Italian violence, of June 1940 in Soho, remarked upon at the time by a curious George Orwell, see S. Orwell and I. Angus (editors), *Collected Essays: Journalism and Letters of George Orwell*, Vol. 2, *My Country Right or Left*, Harmondsworth, Penguin Books, 1980, p. 394,

and also the subject of Lucio Sponza's essay, 'The Anti-Italian Riots, June 1940', in Panayi, *Racial Violence*, pp. 130-148. In order to underline the persistence of hostility in the East End, the major settlement area, one can turn to C. Husbands, 'East End Racism 1900-1980: Continuities in Vigilantist and Extreme Right-Wing Political Behaviour', *London Journal*, Vol. 8, 1982, pp. 3-26.

46 H. Arendt, *The Origins of Totalitarianism*, London, Allen and Unwin, 1958, p. ix.

47 H. Pollins, *Economic History of the Jews in England*, London and Toronto, Littman Library of Jewish Civilisation, 1982, p. 169. See generally, S.D. Chapman, 'The Migration of Merchant Enterprise: German Merchant Houses in England in the Eighteenth and Nineteenth Centuries', *Bankhistorisches Archiv*, Vol. 6, 1980, pp. 20-41. For a personal testimony from a City figure, see S. Japhet, *Recollections from My Business Life*, London, privately printed, 1931.

48 L. Hannah, 'Entrepreneurship and the Social Sciences', *Economica*, Vol. 51, 1984, pp. 219-234, provides a good account on post-war immigration and entrepreneurship. On restaurants, C. Driver, *The British at Table 1940-1980*, London, Chatto and Windus, 1983, carries detail on the post-war restaurant boom and the involvement by immigrants. On the Chinese, see the work of James L. Watson, for example, 'The Chinese: Hong Kong Villagers in the British Catering Trade', in his *Between Two Cultures*, Oxford, Basil Blackwell, 1977, pp. 181-213. There are references to Cypriots in London's restaurants in R. Oakley, 'Cypriot Migration and Settlement in Britain', unpublished D.Phil. Thesis, Oxford University, 1972, as well as in the earlier, more generally accessible, V. George and G. Millerson, 'The Cypriot Community in London', *Race*, Vol. VIII, 1967, p.284. The Italians in London's restaurants appear in T. Colpi, *The Italian Factor*, Edinburgh and London, Mainstream, 1991, pp. 138-43. For one particular success story, see F. Lagattolla, *The Recipes That Made a Million*, London, Orbis, 1978. A recent development, involving Turkish cuisine, was discussed in the *Financial Times*, 8/9 June 1996. On the importance of Soho, see J. Summers, *Soho*, London, Bloomsbury, 1989, especially Ch. 7.

49 Anderson, op. cit.

50 J.A. Jackson, *The Irish in Britain*, London, Routledge & Kegan Paul, 1963, pp. 105-6 notes the continuing involvement of the Irish in the building industry in London after 1945, notwithstanding a growing

presence in other fields of activity. See also his chapter, 'The Irish', in R. Glass, et al., *London. Aspects of Change*, London, MacGibbon & Kee, 1964, p. 299. See also K. O'Conner, *The Irish in Britain*, Dublin, Gill and Macmillan, 1975, pp. 65-6. Finally, note the detail in T. Connor, *The London Irish*, London, London Strategic Policy Unit, 1987, chapter 5, based on 1981 census material.

51 E.J.B. Rose, *Colour and Citizenship*, Oxford, OUP, 1969, pp. 306-8; D. Brooks, *Race and Labour in London Transport*, Oxford, OUP, 1975.

52 M. Banton, *The Coloured Quarter*, London, Jonathan Cape, 1955, chapter VI, a classic study of post-war Stepney. S. Shah, *Immigrants and Employment in the Clothing Industry: the Rag Trade in London's East End*, London, Runnymede Trust, 1975; W.J. Fishman (and N. Breach), *The Streets of East London*, London, Duckworth, 1980 edn., Ch. 4; G.S. Jones, *Outcast London: A Study in the Relationship between Classes in Victorian Society*, London, Penguin, 1984, p. 110, notes the relationship of Jewish immigrants to sweating. On Jewish and other tailors in the capital, see A.J. Kershen, *Uniting the Tailors: Trade Unionism amongst the Tailors of London and Leeds 1870-1939*, London, Frank Cass, 1995. For more recent developments, see also A. Phizacklea, *Unpacking the Fashion Industry. Gender, Racism and Class in Production*, London, Routledge, 1990; P. Marsh, *The Anatomy of a Strike: Unions, Employment and Punjabi Workers in a Southall Factory*, London, Institute of Race Relations, 1967, on the 1965 strike at Woolf's rubber factory. A. Wilson, *Finding a Voice*, London, Virago, 1988 edn., pp. 53-54, on conditions in a bedding factory in Camden Town. 'Goodbye Chop Suey', Channel 4 TV. 22 February 1985, offered a reminder of sweating among restaurant workers. Jackson, *The Irish*, p. 63, 173, notes the conditions under which Irish lived in post-war London. R. Glass, *Newcomers. The West Indians in London*, London, Centre for Urban Studies, 1960, Part III discusses the housing problems of Blacks. See K. Leech, *Brick Lane 1978*, Birmingham, AFFOR, 1980, Ch. 5 on public housing; Foot, op. cit., pp. 210-6 is a powerful voice on racism in Southall in the 1950s and 1960s; Husbands, op. cit., traces the continuity of racism in the East End. Complaints brought to the attention of the Commission for Racial Equality also testify to the continuity of disadvantage.

[53] On which influx generally see P.K. Martinez, 'Paris Communard Refugees in Britain 1871-1880', unpublished D.Phil. Thesis, Sussex University, 1981.

[54] On these refugees, see W.E. Mosse, et al. (editors), *Second Chance: Two Centuries of German-Speaking Jews in the United Kingdom*, Tübingen, J.C.B. Mohr, 1991.

[55] P. Anderson, 'Components of the National Culture', in A. Cockburn and R. Blackburn (editors), *Student Power*, Harmondsworth, Penguin, 1970 edn., p. 230: 'The phalanx of national intellectuals...has been eclipsed. In this intensely provincial society, foreigners suddenly became omnipresent.' Anderson is discussing the period since 1900 but much of his detail relates to the inter-war years.

[56] On E.H. Gombrich see D. Eribon, *E.H. Gombrich: A Lifelong Interest. Conversations on Art and Science with Didier Eribon*, London, Thames and Hudson, 1993. On Popper see his *Unended Quest: An Intellectual Autobiography*, Glasgow, Fontana, 1976 and the obituary in *The Times*, 19 September 1994. On Mannheim there is an accessible essay, J. Floud, 'Karl Mannheim', in T. Raison (editor), *The Founding Fathers of Social Science*, Harmondsworth, Penguin, 1970, pp. 204-13. On Gellner, see the obituary in *The Times*, 7 November 1995. On Lakatos, see R.S. Cohen, P.K. Feyerabend and M.W. Wartofsky (editors), *Essays In Memory of Imre Lakatos*, Dordrecht and Boston, D. Reidel Publishing Co., 1976. See also notices in *The Times*, 6 and 8 February 1974. The role of émigré influences and overseas students in the history of the School is reflected in R. Dahrendorf, *A History of the London School of Economics and Political Science 1895-1995*, Oxford, Oxford University Press, 1995. Apart from the cultural legacy of such individuals, certain institutions can be traced to the immigration of the 1930s. One thinks of the Warburg Institute and the Wiener Library. The immigration of German Jews, both in the nineteenth century and the inter-war years, also resulted in financial contributions to cultural life in Britain, including London.

[57] See S.S. Prawer, *A.N. Stencl: Poet of Whitechapel*, Oxford, Oxford Centre for Postgraduate Hebrew Studies, 1984; W.J. Fishman, *Morris Winchevsky's London Yiddish Newspaper: One Hundred Years in Retrospect*, Oxford, Oxford Centre for Postgraduate Studies, 1985.

[58] On Williams, see the obituaries in *The Times*, 30 April 1990 and *The Guardian*, 1 May 1990.

[59] S. Selvon, *The Lonely Londoners*, London, Allan Wingate, 1956. See the obituary in *The Times*, 14 May 1994.

[60] G. Mikes, *How To Be An Alien*, London, Allan Wingate, 1946. See the obituary in *The Times*, 3 September 1987.

[61] S. Gardiner, *Jacob Epstein*, London, Flamingo, 1993.

[62] *The Times*, 26 August 1989.

[63] R. Davies and L. Ottaway, *Vicky*, London, Secker and Warburg, 1987.

[64] An indication of the importance of the Irish is given in D. Gwynn, 'The Irish Immigrants', in G.A. Beck (editor), *The English Catholics 1850-1950*, London, Burns Oates, 1950, p. 265. For a more cautious view, see G. Connolly, 'Irish and Catholic: Myth or Reality?', in R. Swift and S. Gilley (editors), *The Irish in the Victorian City*, London, Croom Helm, 1985, pp. 225-54. On the Irish generally in Victorian London, see L. Lees, *Exiles of Erin: Irish Migrants in Victorian London*, Manchester, Manchester University Press, 1977, and O'Conner, op. cit., pp. 14-6.

[65] The mosque featured in an article in *The Times*, 22 January 1994.

[66] A. Briggs, *Marx in London: An Illustrated Guide,* London, BBC Publications, 1982, is useful on Marx in the metropolis. At one stage Marx lived at 28 Dean Street above what was to become later one of the best known Italian restaurants in London, Leoni's *Quo Vadis*. The owner of the restaurant at the beginning of the Second World War was interned and has left a memory of his experiences; see P.G. Leoni, *I Shall Die on the Carpet,* London, Leslie Frewin, 1966. The recent purchase of the restaurant by Marco Pierre White will, apparently, result in the name of the restaurant changing to *Marx* (see *The Independent*, 6 July 1996). Alas! If only it were true. Ibid., 4 January 1997 notes the retention of the name *Quo Vadis*. On Trade Union and Socialist Activity among Germans, see Panayi, *German Immigrants*, pp. 190-9, which draws heavily on London. See also R. Rocker, *The London Years*, London, Robert Anscombe & Co., 1956, for the autobiography of an anarchist.

[67] W.J. Fishman, *East End Jewish Radicals 1875-1914*, London, Duckworth, 1975 and H.F. Srebrnik, *London Jews and British Communism, 1935-1945*, London, Frank Cass, 1995. For a personal testimony drawn from experiences in London, see R. Samuel, 'The Lost World of British Communism', *New Left Review*, Vol. 154, 1985, pp. 3-55. The London Irish have also made an important contribution to the development of Labour politics. See M. McDermott, 'Irish Catholics and

the British Labour Movement: A Study With Particular Reference to London', unpublished M.A. Thesis, Kent University, 1979.

68 L.M Palis, *The Blue Plaques of London*, London, 1989. Students of architecture will be aware of the purchase by the National Trust of 2 Willow Road, NW3, which the Hungarian born Ernö Goldfinger designed in 1938. See *Sunday Times*, 5 March 1995 and *Sunday Telegraph*, 2 June 1996. See also R. Elwell, *Ernö Goldfinger*, London, Academy Editions/Macmillan, 1996. On the *Arandora Star* episode see P. and L. Gillman, *Collar the Lot!*, London, Quartet Books, 1980, pp. 198-201.

69 I. McAuley, *Guide to Ethnic London*, London, Michael Haag, 1987, is useful on specific areas and as a general guide.

70 Leech, *Brick Lane*, brings Bengalis and Jews to our attention. See also 'The Promised Land', BBC TV, 22 March 1980. For studies which focus exclusively on Bengalis in London, see S. Carey and A. Shukur, 'A Profile of the Bangladeshi Community in East London', *New Community,* Vol. XII, 1985, pp. 405-17; C. Adams (editor), *Across Seven Seas and Thirteen Rivers: Life Stories of Pioneer Sylheti Settlers in Britain*, London, THAP, 1987; J. Eade, 'Bangladeshi Community Organisations in Tower Hamlets, East London', in C. Clarke, C. Peach and S. Vertovec (editors), *South Asians Overseas. Migration and Ethnicity*, Cambridge, Cambridge University Press, 1990, pp. 317-30. For a wider picture, see House Of Commons Home Affairs Committee, *Bangladeshis in Britain, 1986-87*, London, HMSO, 1987. The continuity of immigration into the East End is such that one observer has claimed: 'In one sense the whole of East London's history as an urban unit could be written in terms of immigration'; K. Leech, 'The Role of Immigration in Recent East London History', *Cosmos*, No. 4, 1966, p. 15. See also C. Bermant, *Point of Arrival: A Study of London's East End*, London, Eyre Methuen, 1975.

71 On Chinatown Annie, see A. Lai, B. Little and P. Little, 'Chinatown Annie: The East End of Opium Trade 1920-35: The Story of a Woman Opium Dealer', *Oral History*, Vol. 14, 1986, pp. 18-30. For the public debates on Chinese and drug trafficking in the early twentieth century, there is C. Holmes, 'Chinese Connection', in G. Alderman and C. Holmes (editors), *Outsiders and Outcasts*, London, Duckworth, 1993, pp. 71-93. On the significance of Gerrard Street, see Watson, op. cit.

[72] Merriman, op. cit., is useful on settlement. See also Holmes, *John Bull's Island*. On Brixton, see the pioneer academic study, S. Patterson, *Dark Strangers: A Study of West Indian Immigrants in Brixton*, Harmondsworth, Penguin Books, 1965, and D. Hinds, 'The Island of Brixton', *Oral History*, Vol. 8, 1980, pp. 49-51.

[73] See T. Kushner, 'Jew and Non-Jew in the East End of London: Towards an Anthropology of "Everyday" Relations', in Alderman and Holmes, op. cit., pp. 32-52. See more generally on this theme, J. Higham, 'Anti-Semitism in the Gilded Age', *Mississippi Valley Historical Review*, Vol. 43, 1956-7, pp. 559-78.

[74] Kushner, op. cit., is useful, for example on locating the history of the Jews in East London to major currents which affected the area. There is also relevant material in Srebrnik, op. cit., J. Davis, 'Jennings' Buildings and the Royal Borough: The Construction of the Underclass in Mid-Victorian England', in Feldman and Jones, op. cit., pp. 11-39 also successfully locates the history of a group of London Irish to the credit, housing and labour networks which exercised a crucial influence over their lives.

[75] C. Holmes, 'Building the Nation: the Contributions of Immigrants and Refugees to British Society', *Journal of the Royal Society of Arts*, November, 1991, pp. 1-8; Commission for Racial Equality, *Roots of the Future: Ethnic Diversity in the Making of Britain*, London, CRE, 1996.

[76] C. Holmes, 'Historians and Immigration', in C.G. Pooley and I.D. Whyte (editors), *Migrants, Emigrants and Immigrants: A Social History of Migration*, London, Routledge, 1991, pp. 201-2, for earlier comment.

[77] P. Cohen-Portheim, *The Spirit of London,* London, Routledge, 1935, p. VII.

[78] R. Porter, *London: A Social History*, London, Hamish Hamilton, 1994, p. 353.

[79] Merriman, op. cit., pp. 62-71, 163-8, 179-84, and 185-9, respectively. Even this survey passes over some groups. It contains nothing for example on the Maltese minority, on which see G. Dench, *The Maltese in London*, London, Routledge and Kegan Paul, 1975.

[80] Hence the timeliness of the conference, 'London: A Promised Land?', organised by the Centre for the Study of Migration, Queen Mary and Westfield College, University of London, on 11 November 1995.

# 3 Allies in the Promised Land: Reflections on the Irish and the Jews in the East End

*William J. Fishman*

*The chapters in this book have been written by scholars who are dedicated to their subjects and who have spent considerable time researching, analysing, and writing up their findings. Rarely do they have the opportunity to play a part in the events that they are concerned with. Bill Fishman is an exception. He is the grandson of an immigrant and the son of an East End tailor who suffered the harshness and inequity of the depressed 1930s. Bill Fishman has lived through momentous times and yet is still able to take the scholar's approach to analysis. The Battle of Cable Street which took place on 4 October 1936 was not a myth to him but a reality which he experienced first hand that autumn Sunday in the East End. He saw for himself the way in which Catholic Irish dockers and orthodox Jews united to fight the common enemy, the fascist blackshirts and their leader, Oswald Mosley. The events of that day drove him to use his academic and literary skills to educate and inform others; to enable them to appreciate that, in the cause of humanity and decency, opposites can come together. It is the reflections of the scholar and East Ender, Bill Fishman, that follow.*

*Editor*

The East End of London has always been a point of arrival for immigrants fleeing from persecution, or seeking a Promised Land free from religious and political harassment, where bread, work and a roof over their heads could be attained in relative security. It was during the 19th century that this influx of outsiders reached a crescendo and throughout the long years a settled security would prove a sad delusion. In this chapter I intend to concentrate on the two ethnic groups that provided the majority of these newcomers, that is the Irish and the Jews.

First those 'troublesome strangers' - the Irish. The English, once having conquered and despoiled Ireland, were, throughout the centuries that followed, faced with a continual influx of impoverished Irish folk, seeking bread and work. They were consistently greeted with suspicion, hostility and harassment. As early as 1413 there was a statute ordering 'all Irishmen and Irish clerics and beggars called *chamberdykins* be voided out of the realm.' There were laws restricting Irish movement within England in the 16th and 17th centuries. In 1629 the City of London protested to the King 'that the realm hath of late been pestered with a great many Irish beggars who live here idly and dangerously and are an ill-example to the Natives of the Kingdom'.

The East End of London, especially the Thames riverside, became a natural habitat for the poor Irish. Located just outside the City gates it was the area of settlement for both permanent and casual servants of the country's financial and trading centre, the boat builders and street sellers and, therefore, a magnet for the Irish labourer seeking a roof and livelihood. Competition for work in the docks, market and local textile trades led to conflict. There were anti-Irish riots in Spitalfields in 1736, in Wapping, the Dock area, in 1768, and in Shadwell in 1786. The latter taking place almost opposite to where Hannah, mother of one of the Founding Fathers of America, Thomas Jefferson, was born. In the first case, weavers protested that the Irish were undercutting their wages. In the second there was confrontation between Irish coal heavies and English sailors, resulting in injuries and some deaths. Only the Irish heavies were arrested - not the English sailors who had instigated the fracas - and two of the Irishmen, Murphy and Duggan, were hanged. In the Shadwell affray, the police descended in force and seven men, all Irish, were hanged! Such was the positive discrimination in favour of the Celt where hanging was concerned.

The Irish writer, J. Denvier, aptly put it as late as 1892:

> We know how, by studied insults to his creed and country, the hot-blooded Irish Celt is often made to appear the aggressor. In any case, he is nearly always the greatest sufferer, for even if he comes off victorious in the fight with his opponents, the law is pretty sure to claim him in the end as the chief victim.[1]

Needless to say this posited an opposite view attributed to a respectable native East Londoner who mouthed the common prejudices that long persisted:

> The quarrelsome, riotous and indeed, blood-thirsty disposition of the lower orders of Irishmen, when intoxicated with gin or whisky, has long called for exemplary punishment.[2]

Yet history recalls that it was those British armies and navies which fought and defeated Napoleon that were filled with Irish volunteers. And it was Irish muscle, sweat and blood that not only build the roads and canals (the *navvies* of the late 18th Century), but also the London docks in the early 19th Century. It was they that enabled the English capital to develop as the greatest and most profitable commercial port in the Western world, and Britain to become renowned as the Workshop of the World.

After Waterloo, Irish immigration into the East End reached a crescendo. The same area had already become a point of attraction for any feckless transient mendicant, loafer and con-man in the metropolis. Soon the residuum of the respectable fled. By the 1850s much of the area had become a dark, nefarious slum, with a network of rookeries containing leprous, one-storied rickety cottages and open middens. Those very houses which had once nurtured the affluent Huguenot silk merchant had degenerated into fetid lodging houses inhabited by a melange of causal Irish labourers, cheap sweatshop tailors, whores and thieves kitchens, their denizens later appropriately titled - 'The People of the Abyss'. The poet Francis Thomson caught the flavour, when, as an insomniac and nocturnal wanderer, he sought shelter in the Catholic Crispin Street Sisters of Mercy Hostel, and recalled the image in his *City of Dreadful Night*.

Professor Scally, in his own learned studies[3] has already perceptively analysed how and why adverse agrarian conditions forced the Irish peasantry to emigrate. Many died en-route before reaching their Promised Land, those that survived having overcome terrible hazards. There was a special factor that brought them to England. As England and Ireland were in law, one Kingdom, there were natural forces compelling the surplus population in Ireland to seek bread and work in the former, especially London. Here the Poor Law operated and, though it gave little and harshly, it still kept starvation at bay. Locally, as already gauged, throughout the 19th century the Irish were a source of cheap labour, particularly in the Wapping and Isle of Dogs area, the dock lands they and their kin had helped to build. After the late 1870s, with local unemployment numbers running high during a great recession, rents rose, with pressure on scarce accommodation assuming dangerous proportions after Disraeli's Artisans Dwellings Act was passed in 1876, ostensibly to replace the slums by local high rise functional accommodation for the 'lower classes'. In reality it meant the demolition of large parts of the East End but *minimum* replacement of new houses to meet the needs of the labouring poor; a factor aggravated by the action of the privately financed Metropolitan Board which brought up the vacant land for speculative deals rather than, for what they *wrongly* deduced, was the less profitable potential from housing the poor! *Plus ca change*...?[4]

As for the Irish, a high density locally led to a report of 2.7 people sharing one bed. A vivid picture of Irish life was given in a contemporary novel *Kate Geary* by a Miss Mason. It tells the story of an Irish girl's arrival in Spitalfields, where hungry and alone she finds shelter in a teeming Irish slum. Here, about a thousand souls are huddled together in the labyrinthine alleys and leprous cottages that form the precinct. Folks are roughly divided into three groups - those in regular work, the casuals who work occasionally, and those who never work at all. 'The first' we are told, 'are exclusively women, generally blessed with a lazy, drunken husband and a large family of small children, all of which they contrive to keep alive on 8/- a week'.

> ...and for this pittance they must rise at five on a cold morning, be on their milk-walk before six, return at eleven and after snatching a hasty meal, which they must prepare for themselves and children, go forth again to their toilsome round, labouring under a heavy yoke, again to return in the evening, exhausted and hungry, to find the hearth cold, Pat at the beer shop, the youngest child fretful, the elder sickening with the measles.[5]

And this may well have been a realistic picture of a more fortunate family.

The first great social investigator of London's underclass in the 1850s, Henry Mayhew, believed, quite wrongly, that 90 per cent of London's criminal class was Irish. For he contradicts himself in his own generalisation of the Irish character. Certainly drunken and tumultuous were many of their men folk, but amongst the East End Irish their mutual concern was great. A newly arrived immigrant would be helped to find a job, or given a loan with no interest charged. In Spitalfields alone, when an appeal went out for the Catholic poor in 1852, contributions from the rich yielded a measly £1 sterling whilst the Irish poor raised £600. Considering that there were about 9000 Irish locally, most of them living on the margin, the £600 collected represented immense sacrifices.[6]

As for the legend of drunk and disorderly behaviour, there *was* a controlling authority. The unsung hero of Irish East London was the homespun priest. Oft times he was both policeman and judge as well as spiritual guide to his flock, the mainstay of moral values. He often imposed his will successfully on any recalcitrant, for he could command instant respect and obedience. There was the famous Father John Moore of a dockside parish, a splendid late Victorian cleric, who conscripted a corps of 500 honorary collectors, each of whom extracted one penny from each of his 5000 parishioners; even better, his successor Father Bill Kelly, a financial pundit, who in the same way accumulated a weekly score of £50; his contributors the regular dockers, artisans, petty traders, and dock and factory foremen. The money would be used to help the poor and needy. And, of course, to help maintain the Church. Masses were compulsory and full to capacity. The income accruing helped to sustain its stability and continuity. In Wapping alone right up to the 1930s, 15,000 and more Irish inhabitants guaranteed the upkeep of two chapels, five schools and five priests.

Yet right up to the beginning of the Edwardian era, when cross ethnic relationships loosened, the existence of their Irish neighbours gave the local Cockney a feeling of superiority, an attitude succinctly put by scholar Dr A.L. Arenstein in his 'Victorian Prejudices Re-examined'.

> Paddy was regarded as a consequence, not of environment, but of centuries old racial inheritance, as a hard drinking, hard fighting, peasant, emotionally unstable, ignorant and indolent...the Anglo-Saxons bred in the forests of Germany were the true carriers of civilisation.[7]

By the end of the 19th century, as the increase in intermarriages resulted in wider assimilation, attitudes changed as the new Anglo-Irish took over areas of the Tower Hamlets. The children spoke in the local *patois* and, as *English* lads and lasses, became the bootless nippers of the East End. It was against this backcloth of a still socially deprived milieu, that first Dickens, and later Arthur Morrison, set many of their classic tales. In 1887 social scientist Charles Booth commenced the *first* ever scientific exploration and record of an inner city deprived area. In Chapter 1 of his *Life and Labour of the People of London* Jewish and Irish immigrants constitute the prime characters. For after 1881 a new, exotic invader entered into the East End; the Jew, fleeing from the pogroms and persecutions of Czarist Russia.

There was already a long settled Jewish community bordering the City, consisting to a large extent of affluent merchants, bankers, stock dealers and lawyers of Sephardic descent. There had been pulses of East European immigration earlier but during the 1880s the influx reached a crescendo. The result was pressure on scarce working class accommodation and, as first inter-ethnic antagonisms erupted, the Anglo-Irish were pressured to move eastward towards Bow and Poplar and southward to their own kind established along the Thames side. By 1889 Charles Booth could report:

> The newcomers have gradually replaced the English population in whole districts which were formerly outside the Jewish quarter...and many streets and lanes and alleys have fallen before them: they fill whole blocks of model dwellings; they have introduced new trades and new habits and they live and crowd together and meet their fate *independent of the great stream of London life surging around.*

It was this ghetto, as much self-created, as externally imposed by an antipathetic host culture, that was bound to create considerable hostility between the new and old 'alien' invaders. In the East End, animosity arose at first from the Irish Catholics' fear of competition as street traders or in the lowest jobs and for scarce accommodation, rather than from religious or racial motives.

For as the Jews pressed eastward, so did their style begin to project a bizarre quality on to the immediate environment. Slowly the narrow streets and cobbled alleyways, once Irish habitations - their previous inhabitants pressured by the newcomers to move towards the docks - filled up with the *landsmanschaft*, families emanating from the same town or village *shtetl* in Russia or Poland. They formed their own self-contained street communities with workshops located in those once stately houses constructed by bourgeois Huguenot merchants and despoiled by the 19th century transient slum folk. On Fridays, the eve of *Shabbat* (Jewish sabbath), the cloistered thoroughfares came to life as candles blazed from the front parlours of the surrounding shabby, three tiered tenements and congested rookeries. During the week they laboured at the tailor's bench or behind the machine of the sweatshops geared to the production of cheap clothing and boot making: the newcomers, *greeners*, sometimes sleeping on those very benches and breathing in the fetid air accumulated during the day. The weekend spelt freedom, when the young escaped from parental restraints to the gay vulgarity of the *Pavilion* or *Shoreditch* music halls, or, more daringly, to the local dance hall catering for a mixed ethnic clientele. Here sex play was more open, and cross ethnic relationships loosely established.

Later some of these initial encounters would end in a mixed marriage. But for the majority, for all these illicit temptations, the young stayed tethered to their people, since, as that great chronicler of the ghetto, Israel Zangwill, records 'whether he married in his old station or higher up the scale, he was always faithful to the sectarian tradition of his race, and this less from religious motives than from hereditary instinct'. Whilst the first born generation viewed themselves with pride as Britishers, the old ones, like Rabbi Shmuel, could 'never quite understand the importance of becoming English. He had a latent feeling that Judaism had flourished long before England was invented.' Like sentiments once expressed by his Irish predecessors, with both experiences leading to sharp, sometimes violent, tensions between old and young, Irish and home born!

For those who had just arrived or were impervious to change and circumstance, the *shtiebl*,[8] like its Irish counterpart, the chapel, sustained their ambiguous response to the new environment. It was a confirmation of their identity in *goles* (exile) yet reflected a poignant attachment to the *heim* (homeland), i.e. Russia and Poland. Beatrice Webb, no sympathiser with the alien immigrant, noted the spiritual and practical needs offered by their *stiebliech.* Even she responded in some degree to the emotional manifestations of the participants.

> Here, early in the morning or late at night, the devout members meet to recite the morning and evening prayers or to decipher the

> sacred books of the Talmud. And it is a curious and touching sight to enter one of the poorer and more wretched of these places on a Sabbath morning.

But it is Israel Zangwill, who was involved and understood, who presents the reality with wit and pathos unrivalled in its imagery:

> The *shtiebl* consists of two large rooms knocked into one, and the rear partitioned off for the use of bewigged, heavy jawed women who might not sit with the men lest they should fascinate their thoughts away from things spiritual. Its furniture was bare benches, curtained ark at the end containing two parchment scrolls of the Law, each with a silver pointer and silver bells and pomegranates. The room was badly ventilated, and what little air there was generally sucked up by a greedy company of wax candles, big and little stuck in brass holders.
>
> Here the worshippers came two and often three times a day to batter the gates of heaven and to listen to sermons more exegetical than ethical. They dropped in, mostly in their working garments and grime, and tumbled and roared and chorused prayers with a zeal that shook the window panes, and there was never the lack of a *minyan* - the congregational quorum of ten.
>
> This synagogue (Sons of the Covenant) was all of a luxury many of its sons could boast. It was their salon and their lecture hall. It supplied them not only with their religion, but their art and letters, their politics and their public amusements. It was *their* home as well as the Almighty's and, on occasion, they were familiar and even a little vulgar with Him. It was a place in which they could sit in their slippers ... for though they did so frequently, it was by way of reverence, not ease. They enjoyed themselves in this *shool* of theirs; they shouted and skipped and shook and sang, they wailed and moaned, they clenched their fists and thumped their breasts, and were not least happy when they were crying. There is an apocryphal anecdote of one of the old ones caught in the act of taking a pinch of snuff, when the confession caught him unexpectedly. 'We have trespassed', he wailed mechanically, as he spasmodically put snuff in his bosom and beat his big nose with his clenched fist.[9]

The immigrants of today, particularly the West Indian exiles in their home-spun Revivalist chapels, would know what this is all about. For the rejected and the dispossessed, the language may be different but the liturgy is the same.

As with the Irish, the immigrant Jew was subjected to both national and local ostracism. With the ebb and flow of economic conditions, he was vulnerable as a *national* scapegoat, conjured up by politicians 'on the make' and even trade union leaders, albeit ill-informed and prejudiced, who viewed their coming as a threat to the livelihood of their members. The result was that, in 1900, was born, in the East End of London, the British Brothers' League, the first quasi-Fascist organisation, whose racist ideology and violent activity against local Jews foreshadowed Mosley's Union Movement of the 1930s. Anti-alien, that is anti-Jewish, immigrant sentiment resulted in the passing of the first Aliens Bill in January 1906. Up to 1914, the influx was reduced to 4,000 a year. When war broke out, immigration had virtually ceased and the East End Jewish ghetto had consolidated itself with numbers amounting to over 100,000.[10]

What of Irish-Jewish relations during this period, that is from say the 1880s to their joint exodus after World War Two? As suggested, after initial tensions and antagonisms, accruing partly from religious and cultural differences but mainly from competition for cheap labour and scarce accommodation, there developed a sympathetic inter-ethnic rapport. First the proximity of those living on the joint peripheries and the common experience of poverty and alienation by their English hosts, drew those who found themselves neighbours in the same street to forge a close friendship, often initiated by their children attending the same Board school; with mutual aid in adversity accelerating the process. Secondly, many a local Anglo-Irish girl found herself working beside her Jewish counterpart in the tailoring and dressmaking workshops which expanded under the aegis of Jewish entrepreneur masters. Thirdly, this, in return, led to common social and political solidarity as Anglo-Irish and Jew combined during parallel strike action. Before 1914 instances of practical mutual aid was evidenced during two major tailoring and dock disputes: the first in 1889, the second in 1912, when Jewish tailors and Anglo-Irish dockers raised money, and in the latter, fought side by side, in support of each other's cause.

The Jewish tailors' strike that began on 26 August 1889, followed in the wake of that month's dock strike. The dockers were not slow to manifest their support for those exploited in the sweatshops of the East End. Comradely platform encouragement was given by such guest speakers as dockers' leaders Tom Mann, John Burns and Ben Tillett. On Thursday 26th September 1889, Miller of the Dock Strike Committee, after the favourable settlement of their dispute twelve days before, handed £100 to Fricke, treasurer of the Jewish Tailors Relief Fund at the tailors strike headquarters in the 'White Hart' pub in Greenfield Street. Militancy on both sides and mutual sympathy proved catalysts for a future common accord between East End Jewish and Irish workers.

1912 proved a watershed in their relationship. Under the remarkable leadership of an exiled German gentile Anarchist, Rudolf Rocker, a third great strike by Jewish tailors ended in triumph, whilst their docker neighbours were poised for their second major dispute. Once again, as in 1889, suffering made strange bedfellows. Rocker was quick to use this opportunity to bring together Jewish and Irish workers. He organised, and spoke at, joint strike meetings, acting as an inspiring force behind combined tailor and docker demonstrations on the Mile End Waste.

Whilst the tailors gained their victory, the dock strike dragged on and dockers' families faced starvation. Rocker, as editor of the Yiddish Anarchist newspaper, the *Arbeter Fraint,* called on the Jewish tailors to rally to the aid of the dockers. A committee was set up between the local Anarchist group and the Jewish Unions, the former providing an elected secretary and treasurer. It called on immigrant families to succour the children and offers of food, accommodation and gifts, more than could be accepted, poured in from Jews, many of whom could scarcely feed themselves. Local retailers subscribed shoes and clothing.

Dockers, other non-Jewish trade unionists and social workers spoke of the warmth and hospitality shown to their unfortunate charges by East End Jews. Rocker and his partner Millie personally collected children from the docks, most of whom were reduced to a 'terrible undernourished state barefoot and in rags'. Over three hundred children were taken into Jewish homes. Such action was in accord with Rocker's aim of uniting Jewish and Gentile workers in their struggles for better conditions globally. It laid the foundations of many cross-ethnic friendships which neither time nor circumstance could erase. The 'hungry thirties' would register their fulfilment.

For between the wars, in the area of political control there emerged no Tammany Hall here. The Labour Party revealed that, by unwritten agreement, the Lanes and Frankels i.e. the 'Cohens and the Kellys', as councillors within the same party, virtually ruled Tower Hamlets. The dockland rhetoric 'No Jews allowed down Wapping' might persist as an empty slogan. For the survivors of 1912 did not forget. It was the Anglo-Irish dockers of Wapping and St. Georges who helped provide the militant vanguard of the anti-Fascist movement, which, on October 4th 1936, at the legendary Battle of Cable Street, forcibly prevented the Mosleyite incursion into Jewish east London.

During the inter-war years the association of Jews and Irish with the area held fast, although some social mobility claimed the exit of hundreds of both to the provinces and newly created suburbs. The main thrust of Jewish movement was eastward to middle class Redbridge, and, for the more affluent, the north west passage to Golders Green. Whilst the Irish who left, went to fill up the new industrial centres on the eastern fringe, such as Dagenham, where they provided a skilled workforce for an expanding Ford motor plant.

The Second World War forced a great exodus on the majority of both and a dramatic end to the local connection. Hitler's Luftwaffe, pinpointed the area as a target, causing widespread destruction of local homes and industries and mass evacuation. After 1945, some did return. But the task of rebuilding our economy meant a greater demand for professionals to be drawn from all social classes. This led to government legislation opening up higher educational and training opportunities for all. The Labour Party in power's drive for a new, more equitable society demolished the old class walls of East London, and the children of both ethnics have fled. Since the 1950s the last bastions of the Jewish *shtetlech* have crumbled, whilst the historic Irish based dock industry has gone, superseded by container based ports elsewhere.

Today, a few surviving ancients, worn out Jewish tailors and superannuated Anglo-Irish dockers wander aimlessly through the new 'alien' streets that have been transmogrified into colourful Bangladeshi enclaves. Their children's integration and assimilation now complete, what can one learn from their East End story. Perhaps, I can, as a finale, offer one lesson. Just as their experience, both as victims, developed into a sympathetic mutual identification as an oppressed minority, so may we recognise that divisions of race and creed should be of no significance whatsoever, in our own appreciation of strangers within the gates.

**Notes**

---

[1] J. Denvier, *Irish In London*, London, Kegan, Paul, Trench, Trabner & Co., 1892, p. 78.

[2] *East London Observer*, 6 April 1912.

[3] R.J. Scally, *The End of Hidden Ireland*, Oxford, OUP, 1995.

[4] For local social conditions facing the Irish immigrant poor see also W.J. Fishman, *The Streets of East London*, London, Duckworth, 1979, pp. 28-46.

[5] *The Rambler*, 1852, Vol. I, pp. 109-10.

[6] J.L. and B. Hammond, *The Age of the Chartists*, London, Longmans, 1930, p. 104.

[7] D.L. Arenstein, 'Victorian Prejudices Re-examined' in *Victorian Studies*, London, June 1969.

[8] Small synagogue or room used as a place of worship.

[9] I. Zangwill, *Children of the Ghetto*, London, Heinemann, 1892, Vol. 1, pp. 254-6.

[10] For further reference see W.J. Fishman, *East End Jewish Radicals*, London Duckworth, 1975, pp. 294-301.

# 4 Leaving the East End: Regional Mobility among East European Jews in London, 1880-1914

*Andrew Godley*

The drama of international migration, with its impact on millions of families, and with lives altered forever, has understandably presented almost a magnetic attraction to historians. Consequently a very great deal is known and understood about why people choose to leave the country of their birth and settle in a new land. However, from the perspective of social science it might be said that the regional mobility of an immigrant population after having initially settled in a host nation is a more interesting, if less dramatic, question. This is because the initial decision to migrate from the country of nativity is very nearly always explained by fairly straightforward economic forces. The dramas embodied in every immigrant testimony of the challenges of being uprooted and having to come to terms with a new and distant land are real enough. But the decision to leave and the choice of where to go is overwhelmingly dependent upon the differences in wage rates and employment opportunities in the international labour market.[1]

The universal adoption of restrictions on immigration among developed economies in the twentieth century indicates that governments and electorates have all been very aware of the simple attractiveness of high wage rates to non-residents. By contrast, the decision to leave the area of primary settlement - the region of a city or a country where first generation immigrants initially reside - is much less well understood. It would appear that this decision is much more complex, dependent on, for example, how the immigrant group responds to the host population after the period of initial settlement and, vice versa, on how the ethnic minority assimilates with the host majority. Once seen from this light the regional mobility of immigrant groups is perhaps much more akin to a barometer of relations between different social groups than any indicator of simple financial well-being. As such it can be seen as a very relevant area of research for the subject of race relations today.

Certainly the general assumption in the histories of the East European Jewish immigrants in Britain has been that they concentrated for many years in London's East End. However, at some stage after 1914, so it is commonly believed, the drift away began and became pronounced so that by 1945 the principal Jewish settlements in London had dispersed north and west and the UK Jewish population was far less concentrated. It is in this way that the East End is believed to have acted 'as a staging area for access into British life'.[2]

The East End was the area of primary settlement in London, a location where important skills, often cultural, could be acquired yet in a social environment which was not so dissimilar to that of the home country. The exact mechanisms of assimilation, or acculturation, are complex and very imperfectly understood by social scientists, but it would seem reasonable to proceed on the assumption that where the cultural distance between immigrant and host populations is great a period of adjustment is necessary before members of the immigrant population can begin fully to participate, and be accepted, in the wider host society. The greater the distance the longer the period. However much it might be wished otherwise history suggests that ethnic minorities are only slowly accepted into mainstream society. An important indication of this acceptance is the ability of immigrants to move freely from these areas of primary settlement.[3]

## Hypotheses of immigrant regional mobility

The regional mobility of immigrant populations to areas of secondary settlement can, therefore, be seen as a very important social phenomenon. But an understanding of how this takes place is dependent upon more than social trends. In particular an appreciation is necessary of the interplay of the economic forces of regional labour markets with the social forces of discrimination and acceptance. There are three more or less competing hypotheses which have been adopted by social scientists attempting to explain the regional mobility of migrants.

The first hypothesis follows the logic of simple economic theory, with the assumption that the forces of demand and supply in the labour market are the dominant influences. If this is the case then immigrants are simply viewed as more workers in a regional labour market. The relocation of any given immigrant to an area outside that of primary settlement is seen as a response to a utility function, where the individual - immigrant or not - is able to earn higher real wages in a different location and so moves.

Such a hypothesis may be criticised for being too simplistic but similar assumptions have lain behind much of the research by the historians of migration and settlement in the United States. In particular, the linking between regional mobility and increasing wage rates has led to the almost automatic connection in much research, over many decades, between regional mobility and upward social mobility. It needs to be emphasised that the simple labour market model does not imply that immigrant regional mobility is necessarily associated with *upward* social mobility. Immigrants may be relocating in response to declining wages and so *downward* social mobility. However, it is a reasonable assumption, at least for the period up to 1914, that most immigrants typically accepted the lowest wages in the labour market on entry and, thus, there was no scope for downward mobility. If there was any social mobility it must have been upward.

This view is not very consistent with the modern (post-1950) migration experience and, perhaps not surprisingly, has its origins in Louis Wirth's 1928 study of the extraordinarily upwardly mobile Jewish immigrants in turn of the century Chicago.[4] More recent research has tended to depict the Jewish experience as exceptional in early twentieth century America.[5] A greater understanding of the more limited degree of ethnic and immigrant mobility in the United States has led researchers to concentrate on explaining why immigrant groups appear less able than perhaps they ought to benefit from increases in wages in the prevailing labour market. The implications of this revised labour market model on immigrant regional mobility has led to the second hypothesis.

The second hypothesis follows the criticisms of the first hypothesis' dependence on overly simplistic assumptions of immigrant behaviour. The assumptions behind this traditional model of immigrant regional mobility are easy to criticise: an excessive emphasis on individualistic behaviour; and a lack of appreciation of the benefits those communal services supplied only in the area of primary settlement, for example. However, a more pertinent criticism comes from the observation of how ethnicity itself distorts labour markets and how, therefore, ethnic minorities are often trapped at the periphery of the labour market as a result of either host-employers' discrimination or immigrants' defficiency in the cultural skills required for employment at the core of the labour market. This core-periphery model has in recent years been developed in order to explain the apparent inability of certain ethnic groups to experience upward social mobility in the United States.[6]

However, the core-periphery model has important implications for immigrant regional mobility. With access denied to higher paid jobs outside the areas of primary settlement, immigrants have little incentive to leave. Moreover, with very few, if any, immigrants leaving for areas of secondary settlement so the costs to acquiring necessary cultural skills for assimilation remain high for all. The absence of immigrants in areas of secondary settlement reduces the supply of intermediaries able to explain and interpret host cultural values to the immigrant group as a whole. This suggests that any meaningful assimilation is potentially denied until the second-generation immigrants are able to act as cultural intermediaries after having benefited from a host-country education. Until this time, therefore, the vast majority of immigrants are likely to be locked into their own regional economy, competing with each other in an isolated regional and ethnic labour market, denied the incentives, never mind the opportunities, to move beyond.

The third hypothesis emphasises non-economic forces and explains immigrant regional mobility more in terms of political or social forces. Jeffrey Gurock, for example, highlighted that much of the movement of East European Jewish immigrants in New York from the Lower East Side of Manhattan - an area of primary settlement - to Harlem in north Manhattan was not necessarily associated with economic advancement but more of a displacement effect, typically arising from the urban renewal of the Lower East Side.[7] This is an important counterweight to the first two hypotheses, because if the regional mobility of East European Jews in London was most strongly associated with the kind of displacement features which Gurock has emphasised for New York, then the migration out of the East End is not likely to be correlated with increasing wages. If out-migration from an area of primary settlement is dependent upon displacement from that area then it will also be positively correlated with municpal, or other, redevelopment and relocation programmes, themselves typically triggered by political concerns over high and increasing localised levels of population density. By contrast, if either of the first two hypotheses is correct regional mobility will be associated with changes in wages: with the first hypothesis the immigrants simply benefit from prevailing trends in general wage levels; with the second hypothesis there is likely to be a time lag between the increase in wages in the wider labour market and an increase in the wage of the migrant population. Then there is likely to be further lag before higher wages and the necessary cultural skills have been acquired for residential relocation.

This emphasis on the cost of acquiring cultural skills suggests also that an expected outcome for patterns of regional mobility arising from the core-periphery labour market model would be for extended chains to be the dominant form of regional migration. By pursuing regional location through extended chain migration the vast majority of those immigrants leaving the areas of primary settlement would have their costs of resettling reduced. This is because they would not have been confronted with having to make a complete adjustment to the host society at one given moment, but rather in a series of smaller steps, each one retaining many features from the home culture, filtered through successive relocations. There is a very considerable body of evidence which now supports the idea that international migrations moved along chains, probably in response to the very high cost of reliable and trustworthy information. Moreover, recent research into the pattern of secondary settlement formation of East European Jews in the United States also strongly supports the idea that information flows along chains of migration were important.[8] The regional mobility of East European Jews in London is, therefore, likely to have been either a more or less complex response to changes in wages or an indirect response to increasing population density. The traditional view of Jewish emigration implies that the motives for leaving Eastern Europe were overwhelmingly non-economic. Emphasis in the traditional historiography of East European Jewry has been given to the political disabilities imposed by an anti-Semitic government and the prevalence of political violence against the Jews in the Pale of Settlement.[9] Irving Howe, for example, suggested that the emigration of the East European Jews was in response to the 1881 pogroms and should be seen as something of a revolution, or a 'collective utopian experiment'.[10] If economic motives were not important in prompting the decision to leave East Europe, it might be conjectured that prevailing wage levels were not likely to lead immigrants to leave their newly reconstructed homelands in these areas of primary settlement. However, recent research has led to a marked revision of this traditional view of the motives for Jewish migration. In particular, the evidence for any kind of direct influence of the 1881 pogroms on the migration movement is thin. Most Jewish immigrants left Eastern Europe primarily because they were poor and thought that prospects were better elsewhere. Of course, as the political environment worsened so it became a contributory factor, but overall we must conclude that the East European Jews were economic migrants, and of a very similar nature to the other mass migration movements of the nineteenth and early twentieth centuries.[11] If they were responding to the forces of the labour market in crossing international borders it can reasonably be assumed that they were open to similar incentives influencing their movements into and out of the areas of primary settlement.

**Testing the hypotheses: Jews in East London, 1880-1914**

This review of the three principal hypotheses behind any explanation of immigrant regional mobility suggests that in order to test any of the three hypotheses an examination of ethnic relocation needs to be linked to the trends in immigrant wages and population density. This implies that it is possible to measure both trends, as well as immigrant regional mobility. Unfortunately such evidence is not immediately at the disposal of the historian. What is known is that the regional migration of the Jews in London took place in the context of the mass migration of Jews from East Europe during the period 1880 to 1914. During this time over 2 million Jews left the Russian Pale of Settlement, Poland and contiguous regions. The vast majority went directly to the United States, but around 150,000 settled in the United Kingdom. In both countries the Jewish immigrants were strongly clustered in the geographically small areas of the Lower East Side in New York and the East End in London. Table 1 shows how this concentration of Eastern European Jewish immigrants developed in London from 1871 to 1911.

The decennial censuses of England and Wales, like any other historical source, are never perfect. The most obvious problem specific to the matter of measuring East European Jewish immigrants is that the census enumerators did not ask householders questions regarding religious affiliation, only birthplace. Table 1, therefore, is actually a record of how the numbers of East European immigrants increased from less than 10,000 in 1871 to over 110,000 in 1911. Non-Jewish East European immigrants were not unknown in England and Wales at this time, although they were relatively few, especially in London. This has led to the convention of assuming that these totals are very close to, and to all intents and purposes, the equivalent of East European Jews.[12] This then represents a very considerable increase in the population of East European Jews in England and Wales, especially in London where there were 55,000 by 1901.

**Table 1: Total East European-born residents in England and Wales, and the County of London, 1871 to 1911, selected countries**

**England and Wales**

| | 1871 | 1881 | 1891 | 1901 | 1911 |
|---|---|---|---|---|---|
| *Natives of:* | | | | | |
| Russia | 2,513 | 3,789 | 23,626 | 61,789 | 69,580 |
| Poland | 7,056 | 10,679 | 21,448 | 21,055 | 36,502 |
| Rumania | n/a | n/a | 734 | 3,296 | 4,293 |
| TOTAL | 9,569 | 14,468 | 45,808 | 86,140 | 110,375 |

**London**

| | 1871 | 1881 | 1891 | 1901 | 1911 |
|---|---|---|---|---|---|
| *Natives of:* | | | | | |
| Russia | 1,065 | 1,778 | 12,034 | 38,117 | 42,301 |
| Poland | 4,229 | 6,931 | 14,708 | 15,420 | 26,119 |
| Rumania | n/a | n/a | 286 | 2,106 | 2,532 |
| TOTAL | 5,294 | 8,709 | 26,742 | 55,643 | 70,952 |
| London as % of England and Wales | 55.3 | 60.2 | 58.4 | 64.6 | 64.3 |

Source: Godley, thesis, p. 40.

This immigrant population was very tightly concentrated into the East End of London. Unfortunately the census does not have a separate geographical category called the East End, but of all of the boroughs in east London the East End could be said to be practically coterminous with Stepney and Bethnal Green.[13] The population of the London-resident East European immigrants living in just these two boroughs was around 90 per cent throughout this period, or over half of all the Jewish immigrants in England and Wales. It suggests also that there was relatively little movement out of the East End, away from the area of primary settlement, before the First World War. Yet by the end of the 1920s it was already clear that a considerable number of London-resident Jews had left the East End. Shortly after the end of the Second World War this became a majority.

There are however a number of problems in using census statistics for these purposes, in addition to the difficulties of equating nationality with religion. The first problem with the decennial censuses is with the aggregate totals reported for East European immigrants. The mechanism for collecting returns was for enumerators to request the information from the household-heads. There were complaints in the 1880s and 1890s that East European Jews were not complying and the enumerators were missing thousands of alien immigrants. Certainly the consensus of the historians of the statistics of Jewish immigration is that the count was short for 1871 and 1881. However, it is believed that the enumerators made too high a compensatory adjustment in 1891 resulting in a count believed to be too high.[14] For the 1901 census the Chief Rabbi of the British Jews and the London Jewish Board of Guardians, both very respectable offices of the fully assimilated Anglo-Jewry, issued circulars in Yiddish and took on additional volunteers to ensure that the returns were accurate.[15] The 1911 total, however, appears once again to be too low.[16] Underenumeration remains a problem to this day and one which disproportionately affects any part of the population which may feel that they have something to hide from official eyes. A significant minority of newly arrived East European Jewish immigrants may certainly have preferred to keep their presence quiet in 1911.[17]

The underenumeration of Jewish immigrants will only affect the measuring of regional mobility if it varied from one part of London to another. Unfortunately there is no way of knowing whether enumerators were more likely to undercount in the area of primary settlement (even with helpers supplied by Anglo-Jewish organisations) or miss the presumably relatively acculturated Jewish immigrants in the areas of secondary settlement (where they had no help). The successive decennial censuses are also less than perfect indicators of regional mobility not because of any flaws in the mechanism of enumeration but because counting heads at any one moment does not encapsulate the flows of people moving in and out of the East End. Finally, economic conditions were improving gradually after 1900 and rapidly after 1909. If regional mobility was a response to increasing wages it might be that the 1911 census is too early an end-point in the measurement of pre-1914 out-migration.

If the successive decennial censuses are not sufficiently robust or helpful for the important measurements of regional mobility to be inferred non-censal sources can be used. Unfortunately here, once again, there are numerous problems. The richest source for historians of the East European Jewish immigrants in London's East End for the period up to 1914 is undoubtedly the remarkable research undertaken under the auspices of Charles Booth's investigations into London's labouring classes and the poor. Whilst this represents, perhaps, the single most important source to the historian of late Victorian East London, most of the original research on the Jewish East End is confined to the mid to late 1880s. Drawing conclusions for the period after 1890 from evidence relating especially to 1886-89 is a hazardous exercise at any time. Given that only about 10 per cent of all of the Jewish immigrants who settled in the East End in the period 1880-1914 had actually arrived before 1890, the Booth survey's findings can only be of a supportive nature in any analysis of regional migration. Later research by Charles Russell estimated that in 1900 there were 110,000 Jews in London, of which 100,000 lived in the East End. Of these, he calculated that 60,000 had been born abroad. If this was true it suggests that at the turn of the century almost the entire Jewish immigrant population of London was resident in the East End.[18]

An alternative source of evidence comes from the collection of marriage records from City and East End synagogues for the period 1880-1914. This is a data-set which has, as yet, been little explored, but once the synagogue civil marriage records have been linked to the related Chief Rabbi's certificates of authorisation to marry according to Jewish means, it is possible to build a large and representative data-set, which links the birthplaces of the bride and groom with their addresses at the time of marriage. This evidence is explained in detail elsewhere but for the purposes of examining the trends in regional migration an initial survey of the East European born grooms in the data-set yields the following results, shown in Table 2.

Table 2 shows that for the early part of the period of mass migration into the East End there was an extraordinary clustering in the East End, with 95 per cent of all East European born grooms resident there. Indeed it is possible to be more specific than that. During the 1880s the East European immigrants were overwhelmingly concentrated in the older Jewish communities on the eastern fringe of the City of London and the western fringe of Whitechapel. There, in Spitalfields to the north of Aldgate High Street and in Goodman's Field to the south, Jewish communities had lived for decades. Yet by the late 1890s the pressure of inward immigration led to immigrants settling in streets contiguous to the earlier Jewish communities but which had previously not been Jewish. Thus, brides and grooms increasingly gave addresses from Mile End New Town and Whitechapel. George Arkell suggested that the Jews had followed 'the path of least resistance' as he mapped their geographical spread through the East End in 1899.[19]

**Table 2: Regional Mobility among East European Jews in London, 1880-1914 - groom's residence at time of marriage (%)**

| Areas of settlement | 1880 -1884 | 1885 -1889 | 1890 -1894 | 1895 -1899 | 1900 -1904 | 1905 -1909 | 1910 -1914 |
|---|---|---|---|---|---|---|---|
| (n) | (24) | (55) | (112) | (148) | (197) | (199) | (117) |
| Primary | 96.2 | 94.5 | 91.1 | 92.6 | 87.8 | 84.9 | 77.8 |
| Secondary contiguous | - | 3.6 | 3.6 | 3.4 | 5.1 | 6.0 | 13.7 |
| Secondary - other | 3.8 | 5.5 | 4.5 | 3.4 | 7.1 | 7.5 | 7.7 |
| Outside London | - | 3.6 | 0.9 | 0.7 | - | 1.0 | 0.9 |

Source: Jewish marriage records database - see Godley, thesis.

Table 2 tells another story, however, which is of the beginnings of the move by first generation immigrants away from this expanding area of primary settlement to areas of secondary settlement. Here we see that the beginnings of the move out of the East End was in the early 1900s. In 1900-04 12 per cent of Jewish immigrant grooms were resident in areas beyond the East End. By 1910-14 over 20 per cent of immigrant grooms were resident in the second-stage areas either contiguous to the East End - such as Hackney and West Ham - or in other second-stage areas of London, such as Hampstead and Maida Vale.

This is a very important result because it suggests that the proportion of immigrants who had left the East End was much higher than ordinarily believed in the period immediately preceding the First World War. The census returns in 1911, for example, suggest that only about 5 per cent had left the East End for the areas of secondary settlement like Hackney and Stoke Newington.[20] That almost one-quarter of the immigrant grooms were not resident in the East End in the period 1910-14 actually implies that a higher proportion of the total immigrant population had moved out. This is because, it can be assumed, the probability of relocating away from the East End was much higher after than before marriage, just as the probability of any individual moving away from a given region increases after marriage.

This has important implications. The traditional view was that the move away from the East End actually took place some time after the First World War, that it was as 'the *children* and *grandchildren* of the immigrants [who] assimilated themselves to the fashions of longer established Jews. [And that] this natural trend was encouraged by higher incomes and the departure to more salubrious areas'.[21] However, if the beginnings of a significant move away from the East End to areas of secondary settlement can be dated to first-generation immigrants in the years immediately preceding the First World War, then, contrary to the traditional view, assimilation was seemingly very rapid for a large group of these first generation immigrants, and this itself perhaps related to economic advancement.

A detailed analysis of the important trends of wage rates and population density in the Jewish East End is, once again, something for which complete evidence is not available. However, it was evident to the Board of Trade in 1909 that Jewish immigrant clothing workers were earning a reasonable wage then, and that this was much more than clothing workers in other centres of the industry. In 1913 R.H. Tawney discovered to his amazement that Jewish immigrant tailoring workers were able to earn high wages because of their very high speed of work and efficient organisation. There is little further information on trends in wages in the other immigrant trades, but the clothing industry and ancillary trades accounted for 70 per cent of Jewish immigrant employment in the East End.[22] Even without recourse to complete information the conclusion at this stage must be that after years of real wage stagnation in the 1880s and 1890s Jewish immigrant workers enjoyed increasing returns, especially in the years immediately preceding 1914.

Measuring Jewish immigrant density of population in the East End is also not a straightforward task for the historian. From the mid-1880s onwards the pressure of space did become a major political issue in East London. Most of the blame was laid at the door of unrestricted Jewish immigration. In 1887 the Board of Trade noted that, in contrast to the rest of inner London, population density was increasing in the East End. In 1892 a confidential report to the Russo-Jewish committee of the British Board of Deputies blamed the immigrants' unwillingness to assimilate into British society for causing such extreme pressures of space in the East End. By 1900 the immigration led pressure on East End housing had given rise to enormous increases in rents and various abuses of tenancy agreements. This was compounded by rebuilding programmes which reduced the numbers of dwellings in the 1890s as local politicians and philanthropists attempted to 'solve' the housing problem of the East End through rebuilding. The increased demand for warehousing in the City also reduced dwelling space. Rents continued to rise until the extension of the underground railway and cheap-men's tickets in 1902. From then on population density fell, rents eased and the problem fell away.[23] Population density in the East End was, therefore, falling a decade before immigrant out-migration became significant. It would seem, therefore, that population density was more dependent on outmigration than the other way round. Thus, the third hypothesis - that regional mobility is the result of political or social displacement, and this resulting from a political or other response to high population density - can be rejected.

## Conclusion

By 1910-14 probably over one-quarter of London's East European Jews were living in areas of secondary settlement, enjoying the benefits of larger dwellings and the sense of having escaped from the East End. This proportion had increased from a negligible share in 1900, according to Russell, or perhaps around one-tenth according to the residences given on the marriage records. Either way this represents a significant increase in just over a decade. Moreover, this was at a time of rising wages. The implication is that outmigration was in response to improving labour market conditions, and, furthermore, given the seemingly rapid response to increasing real wages, that there cannot have been very many constraints on Jewish immigrant residential mobility. This in turn suggests that this population group was assimilating rapidly. Compared to what is known about patterns of Jewish immigrant regional mobility in the United States the results given here suggest that the Jewish experience in London was similar to that in New York, and much more favourable than in Philadelphia.[24]

This does not mean that they were following the individualistic utility-maximising path of the first hypothesis. It is impossible to ignore the weight of historical testimony that the Jewish immigrants faced discrimination from sections of the host population. It is simply that this discrimination cannot have impeded their progress very much. They were, in the terms of the second hypothesis considered here, able to move from the periphery to the core of the London labour market very quickly, as indicated by the beginnings of rapid regional mobility. Moreover, this outmigration from the East End in the years immediately preceding the First World War would appear to have followed the suggested pattern of extended chain migration. Almost one in seven grooms had left the area of primary settlement but only to go to one of the contiguous areas of secondary settlement. This pattern of regional mobility through small steps is strongly suggestive of high cultural costs to assimilation. The results are still at a preliminary stage, but the conclusions are already challenging much of the conventional view of a very slow regional mobility of the Jews in Britain. However, more research needs to be done before the full picture emerges of how and when these immigrants were leaving the East End.

**Notes**

---

1 Recent developments in the study of international migration are ably surveyed in T.J. Hatton and J. Williamson (editors), *Migration and the International Labour Market 1850-1939*, London, Routledge, 1994.

2 L.P. Gartner, 'Eastern European Jewish Immigrants in England: a Quarter Century's View', *Transactions of the Jewish Historical Society of England* XXIX, 1982-6, 297-309, citation p. 307. Also see V.D. Lipman, 'Synagogual Organization in Anglo-Jewry', *Jewish Journal of*

*Sociology* I, 1959; and idem, 'The Rise of Jewish Suburbia', *Transactions of the Jewish Historical Society of England* XXI, 1968.

3 The best study on the history of Jewish acculturation and partial acceptance in the UK by 1914 is D. Feldman, *Englishmen and Jews: Social Relations and Political Culture, 1840-1914*, London, Yale University Press, 1994. This builds on the pioneering work of L.P. Gartner, *The Jewish Immigrant in England, 1870-1914*, London, George Allen & Unwin, 1960 and V.D. Lipman, *A Social History of the Jews in England*, London, Watt & Co., 1954. Also see J. Frankel and S.J. Zipperstein (editors), *Assimilation and Community: The Jews in Nineteenth Century Europe*, Cambridge, Cambridge University Press, 1992.

4 L. Wirth, *The Ghetto*, Chicago, University of Chicago Press, 1928.

5 S. Thernstrom, *The Other Bostonians: Poverty and Progress in the American Metropolis, 1880-1970*, Cambridge MA, Harvard University Press, 1973; and T. Kessner, *The Golden Door: Italian and Jewish Immigrant Mobility in New York City 1880-1915*, New York, Oxford University Press, 1977. Also T. Sowell, *Ethnic America: a History*, New York, Basic Books, 1981.

6 M.J. Piore, *Birds of Passage: Migrant Labor and Industrial Societies*, Cambridge, Cambridge University Press, 1979.

7 J.S. Gurock, *When Harlem was Jewish, 1870-1930*, New York, Columbia University Press, 1979, especially Ch. 2, pp. 27-57.

8 See for example, D. Baines, 'European Labor Markets, Emigration and Internal Migration, 1850-1913' in Hatton and Williamson (editors), *Migration*, for information flows; and E. Morawska, *Insecure Prosperity: small-town Jews in industrial America, 1890-1940*, Princeton NJ, Princeton University Press, 1995, esp. pp. 19 and 28-9; Kessner, *Golden Door*, pp. 130-60; and Thernstrom, *Other Bostonians*, pp. 161-8.

9 S. Baron, *The Russian Jew under Tsars and Soviets*, New York, Macmillan, 1976; S. Dubnow, *History of the Jews in Russia and Poland*, Philadelphia, Jewish Publication Society, 2 volumes, 1918-19; and M. Wischnitzer, *To Dwell in Safety*, Philadelphia, JPSA, 1948.

10 I. Howe, 'Introduction', in D. Berger (editor), *The Legacy of Jewish Migration: 1881 and its impact*, New York, Cambridge University Press, 1983, p. 4.

11 A. Godley, 'Enterprise and Culture: Jewish Immigrants in New York and London, 1880-1914', unpublished Ph.D. dissertation (London,

1993), Ch. 4; also see J. Klier, 'Emigration Mania in Late-Imperial Russia: Legend and Reality' in A. Newman and S. Massil (editors), *Patterns of Migration 1850-1914*, London, JHSE, 1996; and J. Klier and S. Lambroza (editors), *Pogroms: anti-Jewish violence in modern Russian history*, Cambridge, Cambridge, 1992.

12 L.P. Gartner, 'Notes on the Statistics of Jewish Immigration to England, 1870-1914', *Jewish Social Studies* 22, 1960.

13 W.J. Fishman, *East End 1888: Life in a London Borough among the Labouring Poor*, London, Duckworth, 1988. There is a considerable literature on the image of the East End in the late Victorian era. See for example, P.J. Keating, 'Fact and Fiction in the East End', in H.J. Dyos (editor), *Victorian Cities*, London, Routledge, Kegan & Paul, 1978.

14 Gartner, 'Notes', p. 99; Joseph Jacobs, *Studies in Jewish Statistics*, London, D.Nutt, 1891, pp. 20-1; and Gainer, *Alien Invasion*, London, Heinemann, 1972, chapter 1.

15 Lipman, *Social History*, pp. 89-90.

16 A. Godley, 'Synagogue Marriage Records and the Vital Statistics of UK Jewry', Discussion Paper in Economics, University of Reading, 1996.

17 See, for example, G.R. Glover, 'Sex Ratio Errors in Census Data', *British Medical Journal,* 307, 1993, p. 506; and F.A. Majeed et al., 'Using Data from the 1991 Census', ibid., 310, 1995. I am indebted to Dr. Sonia Johnson of the Institute of Psychiatry for this point.

18 C. Booth (editor), *Life and Labour of the People in London*, London, Macmillan, 17 volumes, 1902-3. For a detailed consideration of Booth's survey and Jewish immigration see Godley, thesis; and A. Kershen, 'Henry Mayhew and Charles Booth: Men of their Times?' in G. Alderman and C. Holmes (editors), *Outsiders and Outcasts*, London, Duckworth, 1993; C. Russell, 'The Social Question' in C. Russell and H. Lewis, *The Jew in London: A Study of Racial Character and Present-Day Conditions*, London, T. Fisher Unwin, 1900.

19 George E. Arkell, 'Jewish East London: Notes on Map' in Russell and Lewis, *The Jew*. This famous map was based on household information gathered by School Board Visitors in March and October, 1899, pp. xxxiii-xlv.

20 There were only 3,000 East European aliens in the Metropolitan Borough of Hackney in 1911 according to the *Census for England and Wales for 1911* P.P.1912-13 CXI-CXIII, vol. 9, 'Birthplaces', table 3, pp. 114-75.

[21] I. Finestein, 'The New Community 1880-1918' in V.D. Lipman (editor), *Three Centuries of Anglo-Jewish History*, London, Heffer, 1961, pp. 115-6.

[22] The development of the UK clothing industry and the place of the Jewish immigrants in it is covered by A. Godley, 'The Development of the UK Clothing Industry, 1850-1950: Output and Productivity Growth', *Business History,* 37, 1995; idem, 'Immigrant Entrepreneurs and the Emergence of London's East End as an Industrial District', *London Journal,* 21, 1996; idem, 'Jewish Soft Loan Societies in New York and London and Immigrant Entrepreneurship, 1880-1914', *Business History,* 38, 1996; and idem, 'Anglo-American Comparative Advantage in the Clothing Industry, 1850-1950', *Textile History*, special issue on the clothing industry, 28, 1997, forthcoming.

[23] Gainer, *Alien Invasion*, p. 4. for Board of Trade report, 1887; Gartner, *Jewish Immigrant*, chapter V for Russo-Jewish committee report; Russell and Lewis, *The Jew*, pp. 17ff; and Feldman, *Englishmen and Jews* on high rents; Gainer, ibid.; and Gartner, ibid., on rent falls.

[24] Compare with Kessner, *Golden Door*, pp. 130-60; and Thernstrom, *Other Bostonians*, Ch. 7.

# 5 Huguenots, Jews and Bangladeshis in Spitalfields and the Spirit of Capitalism

*Anne J. Kershen*

The causal factors behind the movements of people have been referred to earlier in this volume. There is no one theory which satisfactorily explains why an individual or a group moves from one place to another and then follows a variety of patterns: settlement, re-migration or, after an intervening period, movement onwards. For some the initial migration might be a life or death decision, for others a test of religious beliefs. For many it has been, and continues to be, a process of carefully weighing up the material pros and cons of what, so often, proves to be a voluntary, yet emotionally, psychologically, and physically testing experience. Whatever the motivation, upon arrival in the receiving society the migrant is faced with the necessity of securing a means of economic survival. All too frequently, and sometimes unfairly, immigrant groups are judged by their perceived ability to succeed commercially in their new environment. The graph of success is often based on past example, as is evidenced by Peach's recent categorisation of post World War II ethnic groups according to the 'Jewish' or 'Irish' model.[1] Success in Britain has been, and continues to be, measured through the eye of western capitalism; the visible creation of profitable and expanding businesses accompanied by social status and a high standard of living.

In order to test the validity of this approach this chapter sets out to explore the economic experiences of three immigrant groups which have settled in the Spitalfields area of London, in successive waves, over the past three hundred years: the Huguenots, the Jews and the Bangladeshis. It seeks to determine how they rationalised their economic activities and whether each - or indeed any - of the three can be categorised under the definitions of Weber's spirit of capitalism. In addition it considers whether such categorisation can provide an accurate assessment of a specific group's *real* success or failure.

Weber's thesis that Protestantism was the pollinator of modern capitalism is open to debate and controversy.[2] Without doubt religion alone cannot be accepted as the spur to the accumulation and investment - commercially or philanthropically - of capital. Temporal factors must be included in the equation. Even if the religious theory were to be adopted, the myopic Weberian adhesion to Protestantism, and more specifically to Calvinism, is hardly acceptable in an era in which western religion in Britain no longer reigns supreme.

Each of the three groups under the microscope is acknowledged as having a collective, if not individual, loyalty to their religion and its teachings: Protestant Calvinism, Old Testament Judaism and Islam. Within the limitations of this chapter I seek to consider how powerful a stimulus religion has been in the accumulation of wealth and the investment of capital. Whilst the Judeao-Christian tradition is one which encourages and honours commercial success, providing this is of benefit to the wider society, Weber suggests this is not true of the teachings of Islam which he considered to be the 'polar opposite of Puritanism'.[3] Within Islam, Weber deems, 'rational capitalism is impossible', it being an occidental phenomenon.[4] Gardner's recent research in Bangladesh has shown that this has not been the case and that there are definite grounds for comparison with the other two groups. A number of returned Bangladeshi migrants who accumulated capital in London and invested it in business and splendid houses in Bangladesh, look upon their material success as an opportunity provided by Allah not only to raise their status but also to 'redistribute alms'; for them poverty was the outcome of 'laziness and stupidity'.[5] With these sentiments, which echo mid Victorian and 1980s western economic philosophy as well as the voice of Islam, the returned migrants demonstrate a reconciliation of east and west.

In order to answer the questions posed above, the framework of examination has to be sufficiently broad to incorporate both poles of the migrants'[6] experience, home and host country. The forces which led to emigration, the so-called 'push' factors, and the migrant's self-perception of that force, cannot be overlooked. This study provides three examples; that of the religious refugee (Huguenot), the immigrant (Jew)[7] and the sojourner (Bangladeshi).[8] External perceptions have tended to view the three hundred years of immigration into Spitalfields as lineal. Has this really been the case? Have the Bangladeshis manifested the same allegiance to the Protestant work ethic as the Huguenots, and the same entrepreneurial ambitions as the Jews? Or have they been satisfied, as one recent observer suggests, to rely on welfare benefit and occasional employment, bypassing opportunities for capital investment and entrepreneurial activity?[9] This latter question poses yet another, one which lies at the heart of the debate: are the Jewish and Huguenot models based more on myth than on reality? Has recent analysis erased the records of hardship and failure from the data base?

In examining the economic history of the three groups a number of factors will be taken into account:

* Socio-economic structure of the native environment;

* Push and pull factors of migration;

* The nature of the immigrant community in terms of race, religion and culture;

* The prevailing economic and industrial structure of the host society;

* The immigrants' ambitions and desires in the context of their self-perception and experience - for these may not always coincide with those identified by the onlooker; and, finally

* The power and influence of external forces of commerce and government which, in the case of Spitalfields, have always been only a stone's throw away.

It is the geographic and historical uniqueness of Spitalfields which provides the starting point for this study.

Spitalfields occupies an area of some 250 acres directly to the east of the City of London.[10] It is, and always has been, a 'place on the edge'. This marginality can be traced back to the Romans who built a wall around their newly created town of Londinium in order to separate those who controlled from those who provided. The visible remains of London Wall have long since disappeared but the division survives. At the close of the twentieth century Spitalfields is, as it was in the late seventeenth century when the first Huguenots began to arrive, a place of poverty and unease. The dissolution of the monasteries by Henry VIII in the middle of the sixteenth century resulted in a scramble for land and the building up of the southern end of Spitalfields by Tudor property developers who recognised the benefits of cheap, jerry building. The district soon became renowned as one of twisting streets and alleys packed with mean, narrow houses, home to religious and political dissidents and the poor. A location that was half a mile from the Pool of London, the point of immigrant disembarkation, adjacent to the City of London, yet free from its restrictions, with a reputation for hosting nonconformity, soon became a magnet for refugees and immigrants seeking economic opportunity and religious freedom. It was an area described by one historian of the period, as 'ripe for colonisation by aliens'.[11]

**Huguenots**

The Huguenots were the first major immigrant group to settle in Spitalfields. They were refugees from religious persecution enforced by a monarch who refused to accept the practice of Protestantism within his Catholic domain. Even before the Revocation of the Edict of Nantes in 1685, Huguenots from northern and mid France sought refuge overseas. Of the 40,000 that settled in England some 16,000 to 20,000 French Calvinists put down their roots in Spitalfields.[12] It was not only religious freedom which beckoned, London offered an opportunity to develop entrepreneurial and technical activities. Many of those early arrivals were silk-weavers from Lyons and Tours who brought to the established, but basic,[13] English silk-weaving trade new ideas and techniques for the manufacture of broad silk and the lustring of taffeta.[14] Others were skilled in the arts of clock and instrument making. The Huguenots were perceived as refugees from the middle ranks who 'founded middle class families of good standing ... shone as merchants or financiers among the luminaries of the City'.[15]

The Huguenot myth is one of the 'profitable strangers', their Calvinistic beliefs and practices encouraging both industriousness and thrift and the use of wealth for the general good, either through reinvestment in business or through acts of philanthropy. However, not all the Huguenot refugees were affluent or successful, there is adequate evidence of mendicity from the earliest period of settlement. Charles II, as well as guaranteeing French Calvinist arrivals their freedom established a Royal Brief in 1681 to help those unable to support themselves. This subsequently became a Royal Bounty which survived in one form or another until 1876. Those with sufficient means founded charities for their more unfortunate immigrant brethren. Whatever the myth, not all the Huguenots 'made it'; the 1753-54 Spitalfields Rate Books record that the parish scavengers spoke only French.[16] The more successful Huguenots were concerned that itinerant incomers should not become burdensome nor present a negative image of the immigrant community. Leading charities required proof of six months residence in England before benefits were provided. This manifestation of 'alien' unease and concern for the image being projected to the native society a characteristic associated with late nineteenth century Anglo-Jewry rather than with seventeenth century and early eighteenth century French Calvinists.

The Huguenots offer an ideal Weberian paradigm, their traits being summarised as 'reverence, chastity, sobriety, frugality, industry and honesty.' Marshall considered the Protestant refugees to be the 'ablest, most inventive and most steadfast', whose 'instructions gave England the right lines along which to work'.[17] And it is largely to their credit that the English silk industry, although subject to the vagaries of trade cycles and tariff controls, enjoyed more than a century of expansion. It was Huguenot silk merchants and masters who, by taking full advantage of the availability of cheap imported raw Italian and Chinese silk, developed the London industry. In the eighteenth century government imposed controls on French silk imports enabled the Huguenots to use Britain's foreign and fiscal policies as tools for the creation of wealth.

In spite of illegal imports from France and the whimsicalities of fashion those early Huguenots merchants and masters prospered. Evidence of this is to be found in the building of fine houses, in Fournier Street and Princelet (Princes) Street, at the northern end of Spitalfields, between 1718 and 1728. Ownership of a 'clean and solid comfortable middle class home' being a religiously sanctioned ideal.[18] A continuum of success can be traced through the generations. For example, the Ogiers family settled in Spitalfields in 1700. They remained throughout the eighteenth century and retained their Huguenot identity through marriage and industry.[19] The Bresson family links were of even lengthier duration. William Bresson's great grandfather Raymond became a naturalised British subject in 1710. As late as 1840, when the silk weaving industry was in its final death throws, William owned 200 looms worth £1 each which he rented out on a weekly basis.[20] Additionally, he owned 'a house with a garden' and was 'in receipt of work when others were not'.[21]

For Bresson and others like him the spirit of capitalism was gradually being eroded by forces beyond their control. In his evidence to the Hand Loom Weavers Commission of 1840,[22] Bresson described the appalling conditions endured by those silk weavers fallen on hard times; living in overcrowded, small, insanitary, airless rooms - airless so that the silk would not loose weight - earning wages which had not increased since 1761. As the Huguenot myth of success was fading so was purity of line, as intermarriage and assimilation added to the mosaic population of London.

To appreciate how, in the eighteenth and nineteenth centuries, Huguenot affluence and poverty developed side-by-side, it is necessary to briefly outline the structure of the silk-weaving industry as it operated in Spitalfields. It is a structure of exploitation of migrant by migrant which persists in Spitalfields to this day. The first link in the silk weaving trade's chain of production was the importer or merchant. Next came the throwster who threw or twisted the raw silk for the weaver; the throwing often given out to homeworkers classified as the 'poorest of the poor' due to their pathetic rates of pay.[23] A master-weaver purchased the thrown and dyed silk and gave it out to the journeyman weaver. When the weaving was completed the master-weaver sold the silk to a mercer, who was allowed up to twelve months credit. Small and large scale masters operated in close proximity, 'small' being between 40 to 100 looms in operation, 'large' as many as 800.[24] It was the merchants and mercers who outwardly manifested the signs of success and who enjoyed the fruits of the industry when it thrived. In the slack they could limit their losses by the instant cessation of yarn purchases.

Poverty and misery were all too often the companions of the journeymen and working weavers, who, with the exception of the most highly skilled, struggled to survive on wages frequently below necessity level. Their plight was not helped by a metropolitan labour pool bloated by the inclusion of child and female labour. As early as 1675, ten years before the revocation of the Edict of Nantes, the 'Frenchies'' practice of undercutting wage rates resulted in riots and articulations of anti-alienism. Following the revocation, the Rector of the Whitechapel Parish Church, Dr. Welton, said of the new arrivals, 'This set of rabble are the very offal of the earth, who cannot be content to be safe here from that justice and beggary from which they fled, and to be fattened on what belongs to the poor of our own land and to grow rich at our expense, but must needs rob us of our religion too.'[25] A somewhat contaminated interpretation of the work ethic.

Conditions in the silk weaving industry began to deteriorate following the ending of the Seven Years War in 1763. The period of the war had seen an expansion of trade, the peace brought with it the renewal of imports from France and hardship. The incomes of the Spitalfields weavers - 50 per cent or more of whom were of Huguenot descent[26] - fell to as little as twelve shillings a week net.[27] Low wages, underemployment and unemployment equalled poverty and riots, as the correspondent of the *London Chronicle* recorded on 18 May 1765 that 'it...be felt in Spitalfields very seriously'. The government's response to the riots was the passage of the Spitalfields Act of 1773.[28] The Act set out to regulate the wages of journeymen weavers specifically, and only, within the boundaries of Spitalfields. Prices for weaving were to be fixed by quarter sessions, entry to the trade was to be limited to two apprentices per weaver and combination was forbidden. In spite of controlling the numbers of those entering the trade the Act did little to help those whose incomes already depended upon it. In 1785 the desperate Spitalfields weavers revealed that their trade 'was declining...for want of employment, poverty and distress are deluging like a torrent', whilst in the depression of 1795 the weavers and their families were said to be 'without fire, without raiment, without food'.[29] 'Poor weavers and their families crowded together in vile, filthy and unwholesome chambers, destitute of the most common comforts, and even of the common necessaries of life.'[30] Small masters pawned goods and equipment in order to survive.

Though the silk trade expanded between 1800 and 1826 the condition of the Spitalfields weavers continued to decline. A number of factors accounted for this. Industrialisation through the use of water as a means of driving the power loom initiated the deskilling process and the accompanying use of cheap, female labour, women were 'employed constantly while the men stood idle'.[31] Some masters moved production out of Spitalfields to where labour could be employed at cheap rates. By 1808, three-quarters of the Spitalfields poor were unemployed.[32] Following the submission of evidence by the Ribbon Weavers in 1818, it was generally concluded that the Spitalfields Act had been 'detrimental' and had served only to depress trade. Though those journeymen remaining in Spitalfields fought hard against it, in 1826 the Act was repealed and French imports freely entered the country.

The death warrant of the silk weaving industry was signed in 1860 under the Cobden Free Trade Agreement with France. The terminal decline began decades earlier. In his evidence to the Select Committee on Hand Loom Weavers in 1834, William Hale described how the repeal of the Spitalfields Act had resulted in 'deep distress and lamentable destitution', with the poor going about in rags; and houses, built in the belief that trade would improve, losing almost all their value as wages dropped by over 50 per cent.[33] William Hale, a silk manufacturer, explained that free competition with overseas had been ruinous: one-third of the looms in Spitalfields were standing idle. The condition of the working people had been degraded, 'the poor rate had increased and those persons who supply them with provisions had been bankrupted. In all 'a great deal of misery and disease...destroys the morals of the people'.

The more successful of the Huguenot immigrants had long gone from East London to enjoy the fruits of their labour in more salubrious surroundings. Of the less successful co-migrant dynasties that remained, some silk weavers moved north east from Spitalfields to the adjacent, but cheaper, district of Bethnal Green, others turned to dock labour, a minority clung on as prices fell by more than 30 per cent. Masters who had enjoyed the separation of home and workshop were forced to move the latter into the former, thus reversing the capitalist process. The descendants of those who had brought their industry from France to England and pioneered its expansion now saw free trade with the land of their fathers put the brakes on their economic future. It was a future from which potential to develop the spirit of capitalism had all but disappeared, and which they now had little power to control.

**Jews**

Though the Irish followed the Huguenots as the next large scale immigrant wave into the capital - by 1851 there were an estimated 150,000 in London - we are not concerned with them here as very few settled within the small area of Spitalfields. In geographic terms the successors to the Huguenots were the Jews from eastern Europe. Though pogroms and enforced military service were a part of the migratory push factor, it was the bleak economic horizon of the latter half of the nineteenth century which exerted the most force. Following the emancipation of the serfs by Tsar Nicholas II in 1861, the economic role of the Jew in the villages of the Pale of Settlement diminished. A process of pauperisation and urbanisation followed and, for all but the small minority of Jewish bourgeoisie, conditions deteriorated. Many were forced to migrate to towns and cities industrially unprepared for the wave of new arrivals. The number of Jews in the cities of the Pale grew dramatically as opportunities for employment decreased; 40 per cent of the Jewish population existed without any regular form of income, dependent on the benevolence of their co-religionists. Following the abortive revolt of Congress Poland against the Russian Tsardom in 1863, the plight of the Jews grew worse. Economic deprivation was now accompanied by political, social and physical persecution.[34] For those who could make it, the only hope for material independence and economic security lay westward, for the majority in the *Goldene Medineh* (America). For a minority Great Britain was the promised land. Exhausted immigrants that landed in London needed to travel no more than half a mile to their first point of settlement, to Spitalfields which, by the close of the 1880s, was considered by certain commentators to have assumed the mantle of a little Jerusalem.[35]

On the surface the immigrants from Russia and Russia Poland bore little resemblance to the Huguenots. Foreign in religion, culture and appearance they arrived at the docks armed with few skills, little or no money and a willingness to work long and hard for the lowest of wages, in the worst of conditions for the longest of hours: in other words a preparedness to become sweated labour if that were the sole avenue to economic advancement. The Jew carried with him the Old Testament philosophy of earthly reward for labour and the right to make a profit, combined with the diasporic tradition of entrepreneurship. Economic activity was perceived as 'part of the totality of man's religious experience in Jewish life'.[36] Hard work was the threshold to financial security, for Jews in the diaspora it was the only form of security. What chances were there for those late nineteenth century immigrants to translate their dreams into reality?

By the late 1870s the industrial structure of East London, with the exception of the docks, was small scale and seasonal, concentrating on the finishing trades or the manufacture of clothing, furniture and a range of small items. Jews rarely sought, nor found, employment in the docks, they became shoe and slipper makers, cabinet makers, cap makers and stick makers. However, the most popular occupation for the Jewish immigrant was tailoring, an association which can be traced back to biblical times.[37] It was a trade which fitted well into the changing pattern of consumption that marked the second half of the nineteenth century. The growth of empire, industry and bureaucracy had improved the earning capacity of the artisan and white collar classes. The working man in regular employment was able to enjoy a new phenomenon, surplus income. As clothes were the barometer of status, one way of demonstrating economic mobility was by the purchase of new, as opposed to second hand, garments. The result was an unprecedented expansion of the London clothing industry.

In East London the tailoring trade was run along pre-industrial, sub-divisional lines. It had grown out of the tradition of old clothes dealing and clobbering in the area around Spitalfields. Production was carried out in unhealthy workshops, often converted from the old Huguenot houses. Workshops were small-scale, the average containing five or six hands employed by a middleman or master. The structure of the East End tailoring trade bears comparison with that of the Huguenot silk-weaving industry. At the top of the chain was the wholesale house, invariably an established English company based within the City of London's boundaries,[38] which gave work out to the middleman or master. Bundles of cloth ready for making up were then put through the sub-divisional system, a process of production broken down as far as it was economically and physically viable. Within the workshop there existed an hierarchical structure. The machiner was the aristocrat, beneath him came the tailor and the presser, the latter by his deft use of irons weighing as much as 25 lb. able to turn a disaster into a success. These men in turn sub-contracted to plain machiners and underpressers.[39] It was an industry that thrived on the lowest levels of wages and skill, on the hunger pangs of the workers and on their dreams of moving out of the overcrowded, insanitary ghetto to that promised land.

It was not difficult for an immigrant worker to set up as a master. Beatrice Potter (later Webb) described how he could use the 'living room as workshop, his landlord or butcher his security...'. A small deposit on the hire system secured both sewing machine and presser's table. One pound purchased the status of employer. However, with depressing regularity the employer of one season became employee the next. Seasonality, recessions, depressions and industrial strife ensured that in the 1880s and 1890s, economic security and success were like water in the desert and the immigrants from eastern Europe the children of Moses: many glimpsed the future, few partook of the fruits.

Unrest amongst the Huguenot journeymen weavers in the eighteenth century led to the Spitalfields Act. The discontent of the Jewish tailors in the late nineteenth century fuelled many a strike and the creation of innumerable, but short-lived, Jewish tailors' trade unions, whose membership rarely rose above ten per cent of the workforce. While the labour pool was constantly refilling with greeners there was little chance of improved working conditions. The entrepreneurial spirit was there but, in the years leading up to the First World War, only the ruthless, or fortunate, few made it out of the ghetto.

One of those who did, who had the perspicacity and vision to turn the dream into reality was Morris Cohen, an immigrant from Russia who arrived in England in 1877, with a 'slight knowledge of ladies' tailoring'. In his evidence to the Aliens Commission in 1903, Cohen explained that when he arrived in England there were hardly any English ladies' tailors and garments were imported from Germany. Three years after his arrival Cohen took his first entrepreneurial steps. Conscious of the growing demand for women's tailored outer garments and aware of the paucity of English ladies' tailors, Cohen made up some samples and showed them to a selection of tailoring masters and wholesalers keen to take advantage of the new market opening up. At that time 'All the ladies' tailoring...was then done abroad, principally in Germany and France'.[40] Within ten years Cohen had opened his - indeed the country's - first custom-built mantle-making factory in Spital Square, Spitalfields. He employed some 180 persons indoors as well as giving work out to other workshop masters. As a result of his initiative the mantle making industry in the East End of London provided employment for over one thousand workers.

Morris Cohen provides an ideal example of the realisation of the spirit of capitalism fulfilling both economic and religious requirements. Not only was he very successful and by the outbreak of the First World War able to retire to Brighton and enjoy the fruits of his labour - chauffeur driven car, elegant home and holidays in Madeira[41] - but he benefited others, far beyond the boundaries of Spitalfields. In 1898 the managing director of Hitchcock Williams, one of the largest wholesalers in London, published a letter which succinctly summed up Cohen's achievements to date. The letter explained that, prior to 1889, the importation of women's mantles into Britain had cost the country an annual £150,000. Cohen's perspicacity had enabled British material and labour to be used for the home and export markets, the latter improving the country's balance of trade by no less than £150,000.[42]

Cohen's entrepreneurial activities did not end with the women's clothing industry. In the early 1900s he bought a number of properties in the East End onto which he built workshop additions. These he rented out to other ladies' tailors. From amongst those acorns the oaks of the clothing industry grew.[43] Amongst those who began their mantle-making days in Cohen's workshops were Alexander Steinberg who founded Alexon, Shyer Green, whose sons created Windsmoor, and Solomon Goldstein, co-founder of Ellis and Goldstein, companies which became the giants of the clothing industry in the post World War 11 years. Morris Cohen died in 1927, the company he founded survived just ten more years until the death of his eldest son. As a descendant somewhat romantically described it, 'we went from rags to rags in three generations'.[44] The spirit of capitalism burned bright with Morris Cohen and then, as with some of his Huguenot predecessors, gradually faded as other individuals and events took control.

Amongst the immigrant arrivals of the late 1870s and 1880s Cohen's accelerated success story is rare. For most of the closing decades of the nineteenth century the country's economy was in recession. Life was harsh for the unskilled and semi-skilled who suffered irregular wages and under, if not un-employment. However, as shown elsewhere in this volume, by the first decade of the twentieth century a minority of Jewish tailoring workers were earning 'a reasonable wage', whilst a fortunate few were earning 'high wages'.[45] By the close of the first decade of the twentieth century the movement away from Spitalfields had begun. The Jewish exit from the East End accelerated during the inter-war years. Some left due to the tough anti-alien controls imposed by London County Council, which restricted the provision of housing and jobs to aliens in the wake of the xenophobia and anti-Bolshevism that came with the peace. Others responded to the call of the suburbs now sprouting up to the north west and east of London. Willesden, Golders Green, Edgware and Ilford had become the promised land.

## Bangladeshis

Out-migration in the 1920s and 1930s coupled with the blitz resulted in the demise of the Jewish East End. By the 1960s only a remnant of elderly Jewish residents remained. In Spitalfields, economic transition accompanied domestic change. Type of garment, production method and location all underwent changes during the 1950s. By the late 1960s much of the tailoring and dress trade had departed from Spitalfields and the insanitary sweatshops had become unhealthy leatherwear workshops. The transition coincided with the arrival of the third major wave of Spitalfields immigrants.

There had long been a tradition of men from the region of Sylhet, in the north eastern corner of India, working as *lascars* on British merchant vessels and jumping ship to find short term employment in London's East End: a seamen's hostel for Indian sailors existed there in the eighteenth century.[46] In the 1920s a Sylheti opened one of the first Indian restaurants in the capital, whilst a fellow countryman opened a cafe in Sandys Row, east London in 1938.[47] Before the outbreak of the Second World War, Sylheti seamen seeking work ashore often found jobs, and sometimes lodgings, in Jewish tailoring workshops in Spitalfields. At a time of heightened anti-alienism Jewish employers and their families were sympathetic to others who, like themselves, were subjected to fascist threats and violence.[48] Did those pioneers anticipate that, within fifty years, Sylhetis would have formed the largest ethnic community in the area?

During the 1950s and early 1960s the combination of limited economic opportunity at home and perceived job availability in Britain encouraged young men from Sylhet, to travel west 'Across Seven Seas and Thirteen Waters'.[49] The intention was not long term emigration but short term residence which would offer an opportunity for young, single male sojourners to obtain employment which would provide money to send home plus the chance to accumulate capital which would support them and their families on their return.[50] Those that made the journey were not from the poorest families, but from those who could afford to lose a breadwinner for the benefit of future rewards. It was quite common for families, or even sometimes a small village community, to pool their economic resources in order to sent one or more young males to the *bidesh*.[51] It was an opportunity to acquire a job, save money and return home 'as rich men of high status'. Along with that opportunity came a long-term commitment to one's kin and one's village. Close contact is maintained between the Sylheti village and the Spitalfields community, the politics of one at times indivisible from the other. Land ownership in the north eastern corner of Pakistan, which became Bangladesh in 1971 after a bloody and bitter civil war, was, and continues to be, the determinant of status; to 'labour on another man's land is humiliating and associated with low social position'.[52] In one of the most overcrowded and impoverished countries in the modern world migration is perceived as the only route to upward mobility.[53]

In the decade following the end of World War II the British government followed a policy of encouraging, at times overtly recruiting, overseas labour. It was not easy for east Pakistanis (Sylhetis) to obtain passports for the UK - the Pakistani government preserved that privilege for those from the west of its country - but during the 1950s a small number of Sylhetis found their way to London's East End as well as to the textile factories of the midlands and the north. The Sylhetis are a syncretic Muslim people living an agrarian, pre-industrial existence with few signs of entrepreneurial activity. The young men were poorly educated, had few skills and little experience of the harshness of urban industrial life. On arrival in London they found themselves living in overcrowded male ghettos taking up employment in a variety of previously unknown trades. Life in the *bidesh* did not bring comfort and immediate riches, but, initially, it did bring a regular income and the ability to send home the remittances which 'play a vital part in the macro-economic viability of Bangladesh'.[54] Remittances soon became a central part of the native household budget,[55] an income which those left behind came to depend upon. Money or gifts enabled kin back home to demonstrate their and the sojourner's raised status through house improvements, land purchase, the opening of a business or a more generous marriage dowry. Those villages which were enjoying the benefits of their émigré kin soon became known as *Londoni* to distinguish them from the less fortunate.

The conditions which enabled some of the earliest migrants to return home within a few years were short lived. By the early 1960s Britain's socio-economic climate was changing. The influx of New Commonwealth citizens in the years following 1948 led to heightened racial sensitivity and tensions as the job market contracted.[56] The outcome was the passage of the Commonwealth Immigrants Act of 1962 which stipulated that only Commonwealth citizens with Ministry of Labour employment vouchers could enter the country as primary migrants. Ironically, what was intended as a mechanism for control created the impetus for a rush of Sylheti migrants who wanted to get into Britain before it was too late. For a short period of time labour vouchers were readily forthcoming from relatives and fellow villagers already working in London and the provinces, from prospective employers and from Bangladeshi brokers, in both home and host countries, who promoted and organised migration.[57] At no time was the movement westwards perceived as a permanent departure from the Indian sub-continent. It was a journey overseas that would enable the sojourners to transform their part of Sylhet into the promised land.

The reality was far from the dream. As the 1960s sank into recession, men who had arrived with no experience of an urban economy struggled to survive on the residue of the small sums of money being sent home as job prospects, particularly in industry, declined and employment narrowed. Hopes of early return faded and the process of reuniting families began. It has proved a long, as yet still incomplete, drawn out affair aggravated by the cost of transporting wives and children, shortage of family accommodation in the male ghettos, and always the need either to visit wives and children in, or to send money back to, Sylhet.

As in the eighteenth and nineteenth centuries, the face of Spitalfields began to change as the new immigrants moved in, some having come directly from Bangladesh, others moving south after suffering redundancy in the midlands. All sought homes and employment, as so many had done before, at the eastern edge of the capital city. By 1991, 23 per cent of all Bangladeshis in Britain were living in Tower Hamlets.[58] Spitalfields at the end of the twentieth century houses a Bangladeshi population of 36,000 of which 95 per cent come from Sylhet.[59] What economic opportunities awaited the Bangladeshi arrivals, untutored in the ways of urban entrepreneurial activity? Some, responding to the growing demand for ethnic food, found employment in, or opened, Indian restaurants. Others not keen to distance workplace and home sought economic survival as in centuries past, in the omnipresent clothing trade, albeit now of a different fabric.

Furriery had been another trade pursued by Jewish immigrants in Spitalfields. The trade began to decline in the early 1960s and middle-aged furriers turned to leather manufacture, the fashion rage. But there was a need for new blood, as the traditional pattern of business transfer from father to son no longer pertained. Medicine, law and accountancy were now favoured above the 'rag trade'. Initially, successors were found from amongst the small Pakistani community whose roots lay, not in Sylhet, but in the region of Mirpur. Many had lost their land in the partition of 1947 and, encouraged by the Pakistani Government of the 1950s, travelled to Britain. Those early arrivals displayed an eagerness to accept the challenge and train in the skills of cutting and machining which would enable them to take over existing companies and establish new ones. The first Pakistani owned leather business in Spitalfields dates from 1957.[60] They soon exhibited entrepreneurial keenness, becoming masters instead of workers, and the leather trade enjoyed a rapid expansion. It is in these Spitalfields leather garment workshops that the Bangladeshi immigrants find low paid, unskilled employment in an industrial structure which mirrors that of the tailoring trade one hundred years ago.

The leather industry operates along the age old sub-divisional lines: wholesalers and middlemen - in this instance, mainly Pakistanis - give work out to small-scale workshops (cut, make and trim, known as CMT) run by Bangladeshis who employ their fellow countrymen as sweated labour. Rates of pay are low, even when the Wages Council existed they were usually below the poverty line. Unlike the Jewish experience,[61] trade union membership is negligible and organised opposition to exploitative fellow Bangladeshis rare. As in the times of the Huguenots and the Jews, the clothing industry is ever susceptible to the peaks and troughs of the economy. The recession of 1988 affected the leather trade severely and significantly increased the number of unemployed Bangladeshis. At this point the mirror image hazes over. Unlike earlier times the modern welfare state subsidises the poorly paid or unemployed worker. There is a tacit acceptance of the current pattern of economic activity; welfare, bolstered from time to time by workshop employment. As this tends to operate in the informal economy using both legal and illegal immigrant labour there is little overt opposition to low wages and poor conditions.[62]

Unemployment amongst the Bangladeshi community currently is high, the most recent report estimating that it stands at 43 per cent.[63] There is little evidence of female participation in the depressed East End economy.[64] The 1991 Decennial Census showed that only 13.6 per cent of Bangladeshi females of working age were economically active, religious mores and language being the major barriers. In general, Bangladeshi males seem reluctant to take on the role of the Spitalfields entrepreneur. There are just three Bangladeshi wholesale leather manufacturers in the area, the remainder being Pakistani.

However, there are examples of entrepreneurial activity to be seen in the streets of Spitalfields, particularly along its two main arteries, Brick Lane and Commercial Street. There are innumerable Indian (Sylheti) owned and run restaurants, one of the most successful being 'Shampan', whose owner is reputed to be a millionaire. The catering trade attracts both school leavers and those prepared to work after the school-day has ended.[65] Food emporiums, clothes shops and travel agencies, satisfying the need for regular return and the carriage of remittances, open and close, their survival determined not only by the ability and initiative of their Sylheti owners but also by the vagaries of the national and local economy. Scattered amongst the examples of small scale entrepreneurship are large leather emporiums run by Bangladeshi entrepreneurs who cut their teeth in the urban economy of Dhaka and Chittagong as opposed to the rural outback of the villages. They manifest the trappings of capitalist success, but for the majority it is still early days.

The Bangladeshi immigrant community is still in its infancy, having been present in Spitalfields for little more than twenty years, and those pitted by economic recession. The older members of the economically active male workforce stem from a rural background, enjoyed little or no education and still look to Sylhet as home and Spitalfields as the place of sojourn. However, this is beginning to change as concepts of *desh*[66] and *bidesh* become confused as families are united and elders join sons and daughters in London. Some returned migrants have re-migrated to London, having discovered they no longer fit into rural village life.

It is to the next generations that we must look when allocating role models. The late twentieth century Spitalfields Bangladeshi community is young, 33.6 per cent are aged between five and 16, and there are few of pensionable age. Will they exhibit a spirit of capitalism? Past reports have revealed low levels of academic achievement, high levels of youth unemployment, reluctance to train for skilled or semi-skilled jobs, drug dependency and dealing.

There are those who blame these weaknesses on ethnicity but the resolution must lie in a regenerated local economy, clearly defined career opportunities and a weakening of the drug culture. But things are changing: the Director of Education for the London Borough of Tower Hamlets in a recent report (September 1996) highlights the way in which pupils in the Bangladeshi group are, by the age of 16, dramatically pulling ahead of their African Caribbean and English/Scottish/Welsh peers.[67] Figures for student admission to London University's Queen Mary and Westfield College, one and one half miles to the east of Spitalfields include 173 Bangladeshis currently registered as undergraduate students.[68] A local social worker[69] reports signs of small scale entrepreneurial activity amongst the younger - first or second generation English born - members of the community who are setting up shops, opening restaurants and running CMT tailoring units. Yousuf Choudhury, one of the earliest Bangladeshi arrivals in Britain, believes that there is now a 'strong entrepreneurial spirit amongst the Bangladeshis in Spitalfields'.[70]

## Conclusion

This examination of the Huguenots, Jews and Bangladeshis has perforce been brief. However there is sufficient evidence to draw certain conclusions regarding the fashioning of their early economic profiles. In spite of the differences in time there are common threads. Each group was perceived as 'alien' upon arrival, spoke a different language and worshipped God in varying degrees of difference. All have occupied the same space, Spitalfields, an area which remains constantly under threat from incursion by the City, the immigrant, poverty and deprivation. The pre-industrial economic structure survives and still acts as a magnet to unskilled aliens. A starting point for some and a graveyard for others.

How do we summarise the economic experience of the three groups in Spitalfields? The Huguenot refugees brought with them the sophisticated expertise and labour which facilitated the expansion of the fundamental British silk industry at a time when it was politically viable and economically beneficial for the host society. The Calvinist work ethic encouraged, indeed, advocated, rational economic activity, capital investment and reinvestment using formally free labour. The end goal was not a vulgar expression of wealth but glorification of God through good works and achievements. Yet interwoven with the Huguenot success story and the advantages enjoyed by those who brought with them a skilled, disciplined, educated and financially secure background are the tragedies of failure, poverty and hunger suffered by exiles who carried little baggage, and were forced to survive on charity and the lowest levels of wages. In the Huguenot story the successful and the perspicacious moved on from the first point of settlement. Those that remained, through choice or need, fared less well. All, in spite of their supposed Protestant work ethic, were at the mercy of the more powerful forces of war and peace and the policies that accompanied those two societal conditions.

It should not be forgotten that the Huguenot refugees were just that, individuals and families seeking refuge with little or no thought of return. Denied the opportunity to worship as they chose, they cut themselves off from the past. When, following the Revolution almost one hundred years later, freedom to worship in the land of their forebears was re-instituted, few if any chose to return. They had found their promised land.

The eastern European Jews who settled in Spitalfields at the end of the nineteenth century were poor immigrants who sought an economic future and independence far away from a Tsardom which offered them nothing but alienation and diminishing economic opportunity. In spite of having left families in the *stetls*[71] and towns, few had return on the agenda.[72] There was no going back, for what was there to return to in a land in which they would be forever alien, denied freedom of speech, land ownership and capital acquisition? The *Talmud*, which elevated a trade and business above agricultural labour, taught that there would be adequate rewards for hard work and that profit was a means of honouring the Lord. This directive was to be put to the test in the promised land which, for the many was New York; for between 100,000 and 150,000[73] it was London.[74] The migrant Jew carried the experience of thousands of years in a diaspora where material acquisition was the only form of security. Weber acknowledged this when he wrote, 'National or religious minorities which are in a position of subordination...are likely through voluntary or involuntary exclusions of political influence to be driven with peculiar force into economic activity and seek recognition in this field...'.[75]

Whatever the illusion, the reality of that early eastern European Spitalfields experience was for most, hardship and exploitation. A graphic description of life in 1907, which appeared in the Yiddish newspaper, *Arbeiter Fraint*, tells all:

> It is heartbreaking to see how people, fathers of children, workers, good craftsmen work, so hard, such long hours with heads bent, tremble for their bosses, the majority caterers, shoe makers or drivers and all for what, for a slice of bitter bread in the busy time barely just to keep alive and, in the slack time so little....[76]

The Morris Cohens were indeed rare.

The Bangladeshi arrivals of the late 1960s and early 1970s followed a religion that is eastern, submissive and supposedly lacking the directive of a work ethic. This belief, as suggested above, is open to debate and dispute. The Islamic insistence that 'Allah helps them that help themselves', provides an incentive to capital acquisition as a means of benefiting self and community. And that is what the sojourners of the 1960s came to do. They did not see themselves as either immigrants or refugees, except for those seeking political asylum, their stay was to be short, followed by a return home as rich men. Perhaps this explains why the opportunity to take over the running of Spitalfields leather businesses was rejected.[77] The plan was to save and send remittances home to facilitate that return. Economic and social reality moved the goalposts and it is the children of those early immigrants who are now caught in a vacuum between two cultures. Children who are growing up in one of the most deprived areas of Britain, children whose parents still look to Sylhet as their home and who do not prize an English education and vocational studies above the traditional Sylheti family life. Instead they create educational lacunae by taking their children back on extended visits which can last for a year or more. But the children do not want to return to a land which is foreign in culture and climate, they see their future in London and because of this, their route to, and measure of, success will be of a very different nature to that of their parents.

The myth of success has been ascribed to the Huguenots and the Jews but, as we have seen, this was not always the case. It is far too early to tell what myth will be laid at the door of the Bangladeshis, though according to recent evidence, some are already following the Jewish path out to the suburbs via 'Newham, Redbridge and even Golders Green';[78] an emergent pattern which contradicts the currently projected image of failure and lethargy. Thus it is much too soon to identify a role model. And when choosing that model caution should be exercised in pinpointing the calendar position. We have seen that in reality not each and every Huguenot and Jew 'made it'. External factors such as trade barriers, economic recessions, wars and immigration controls, possibly even welfare benefit, have been the arbiters of what a capitalist society deems 'success'. Within these limitations religion has played, and continues to play, an influential, but not total, role. The rise of capitalism was not simply an outcome of the Old Testament and Protestantism, nor were the outward displays of status seen in Sylhet achieved solely as a result of dedication to the teachings of Allah. The other factors identified at the outset of this chapter must be included in the analysis. The economic structure and history of their native environments clearly advantaged Huguenots and Jews while the rural economy in Sylhet did little to prepare its young men for an urban existence. In spite of their being the 'Spitalfields greeners' of the twentieth century, the early arrivals knuckled under and found work in whatever trades offered employment, the fruits of their labour on view in the *Londoni* villages not the London streets. The host economy which benefited migrant Huguenot silk merchants and weavers upon their arrival also provided an incentive for a minority of late nineteenth century aliens, including Morris Cohen, though it ravaged others. In more recent times, the late twentieth century decades of boom and bust have done little to help those

Bangladeshis who sought a direct route to status, riches and a return to Sylhet.

It is not only the debate surrounding the Weberian Protestant work ethic which comes over in the story of the Huguenots, Jews and Bangladeshis of Spitalfields. The thoughts of an earlier thinker, Niccolo Machiavelli, should be allowed an airing. In his sixteenth century treatise, *The Prince*, he wrote 'Fortune, as it were, provided the matter but *they* gave it its form'.[79] The successful Huguenots of the eighteenth century and Jews of the late nineteenth and early twentieth centuries recognised fortune and gave it form in Spitalfields. However, for the early Bangladeshi sojourners perhaps fortune was not perceived as a leather factory in Brick Lane, but a house and land in Sylhet. For the reality and the myth of the twentieth century Bangladeshi economic experience we must bide our time.

When we come to assess the economic achievements of migrant groups our analysis must be sufficiently broad-based. the 1990s it is a visit to the *Londoni* villages of Bangladesh as well the streets of Spitalfields that provides the markers of success, of nettle-grasping, which enables comparison with centuries past. If the evidence is weighed it would appear that the Huguenots, Jews and Bangladeshis have each rationalised their economic activities. Their rationales are imbued with more than just religious idealism; they have accommodated material and cultural realities and by so doing, redefined the promised land.

**Notes**

---

1 C. Peach, *Ethnicity in the 1991 Census*: *Vol. 2*, London, HMSO, 1996, pp. 15-6.

2 For different disciplinary debates on the validity of the Protestant Work Ethic see H. Lehmann and G. Roth (editors), *Weber's Protestant Work Ethic: Origins, Evidence and Contexts*, Cambridge, CUP, 1995.

3 B. Turner, *Weber and Islam*, 1974, quoted in K. Gardiner, *Global Migrants*, Oxford, OUP, 1995, p. 234.

4 M. Weber, *The Protestant Work Ethic and the Spirit of Capitalism*, London, Unwin, 1938, p. 171.

[5] K. Gardiner, op.cit., p. 235.

[6] In the context of this chapter I use the word 'migrant' to describe a person who moves from one place to another, to settle in a new place - in this instance a foreign land - but *who may not necessarily* intend that move to be permanent.

[7] The perception of the causal factors for the movement of eastern European Jews in the last quarter of the nineteenth century varies; some suggest that it was a direct response to the harshness of the pogroms and limitations on political and religious freedoms. In reality the major push came from shrinking economic opportunity combined with a belief in the promised land.

[8] It must be remembered that this study concentrates on Bangladeshi migrants who arrived between the late 1950s and late 1960s.

[9] I have been asked not to disclose the source of this comment which was made in April 1996 and which will be challenged in this chapter.

[10] Though Spitalfields has existed as an area since medieval times its history as a hamlet dates from an Act of Parliament passed in 1720.

[11] H.L. Smith, *History of East London*, Macmillan, London, 1939, p. 140.

[12] N. Merriman (editor), *The Peopling of London*, London, Museum of London, 1993, p. 245.

[13] The origins of the silk weaving trade are attributed to the Flemings, who introduced the simple process of ribbon making.

[14] M. Dorothy George, *London Life in the Eighteenth Century*, London, Penguin, 1992 edition, p. 178.

[15] Quoted in C. Holmes, *John Bull's Island*, London, Macmillan, 1988, p. 7.

[16] F.H.W. Sheppard (editor), *Survey of London*, Vol. XXV11, London, Athlone Press, 1975, p. 4.

[17] A. Marshall, *Elements of Economics*, London, Macmillan, 1946 edition, p. 11.

[18] According to Weber such a property ownership was 'not an ostentation'. See M. Weber, op.cit., p. 171.

[19] M. Keating, unpublished B.A. dissertation, '19 Princelet Street - a look at Spitalfields 1720-1870', QMW, 1990.

[20] Report on the Hand Loom Weavers, PP 1840, Vol. XX111 p. 715.

[21] Ibid.

[22] Ibid.

[23] M. Dorothy George, op.cit., p. 185.

[24] Ibid.

[25] H.L. Smith, op.cit., p. 92.
[26] L.D. Schwarz, 'Conditions of Life and Work in East London, 1770-1815', unpublished D.Phil Thesis, University of Oxford, 1976, p. 31.
[27] Minutes of Evidence of the Petition of the Ribbon Weavers, 1818, IX, Indust. Rev. Textiles 4, IUP edition, p. 147.
[28] This was extended in 1792 to include those working in the manufacture of silk mixture and again in 1801 to include women.
[29] George, op.cit., p. 187.
[30] Quoted in E.P. Thompson, *The Making of the English Working Class*, London, Penguin, 1968 edition, p. 157.
[31] Select Committee on Hand Loom Weavers 1834-1835, BPP Indus. Rev. 7, IUP, p. 4. analysis of evidence.
[32] Second Report of the Committee of the Lotteries 1808, p. 205.
[33] Select Committee on Hand Loom Weavers 1834-35, BPP Indus. Rev. 7, IUP, p. 4. analysis of evidence.
[34] A.J. Kershen, *Uniting The Tailors*, London, Frank Cass, 1995, pp. 9-10.
[35] One of those was Charles Booth, whose revelatory first volume of *Life and Labour of the People of London*, devoted to East London, appeared in 1889.
[36] E. Zipperstein, *Business Ethics In Jewish Law*, New York, Ktav, 1993, p. 22.
[37] The *Torah* stated that the product of a plant and an animal must not be mixed. Therefore an orthodox Jew went to a clothing maker/tailor who understood the religious requirements of *shatnes*.
[38] For example the company of Hitchcock Williams, based in St. Paul's Churchyard, which remained in business until the mid 1980s.
[39] A.J. Kershen, op.cit., Chapter 3.
[40] *Royal Commission on Aliens*, 1903, PP 1903, X, q 18968.
[41] The author is grateful to Morris Cohen's family, particularly Clive Moss, for providing this biographical detail.
[42] *Jewish Chronicle*, 22 April, 1898.
[43] A.J. Kershen, op.cit., 1995, pp. 102-104.
[44] Clive Moss in conversation with the author, December 1994.
[45] See A. Godley in this volume, Ch. 4.
[46] R. Visram, *Ayahs, Lascars and Princes*, London, Pluto, 1986, p. 39.
[47] Y. Choudhury, *The Roots and Tales of Bangladeshi Settlers*, Birmingham, 1993, pp. 70 and 77.
[48] Ibid., p. 70.

[49] The title of Caroline Adams' book which recounts the history of the early settlers from the area of Sylhet. See C. Adams, *Across Seven Seas and Thirteen Waters*, THAP, London, 1987.

[50] First Report from The Home Affairs Committee, *Bangladeshis in Britain*, Session 1986-87, Vol. 1, p. 9.

[51] The Sylheti word for foreign land.

[52] K. Gardner, op.cit., p. 39.

[53] The population of Bangladesh in 1994 was estimated to stand at 116 million, life expectancy is 47, with 100 women dying every day in childbirth. Adult literacy is less than 25 per cent and 70 per cent of the population is aged under 30.

[54] M. Islam, 'Bangladeshi Migration: An Impact Study', in R. Cohen, *Cambridge Survey of World Migration*, Cambridge, CUP, 1995, p. 362.

[55] Recent figures which cover the periods 1991-2 and 1992-3 estimate the overall inflow of remittances to Bangladesh to be approximately 800 million dollars. These figures take account of migrants all over the world, not just the U.K. from which recently the remittance figure has been reducing. M. Islam, 'Bangladeshi Migration: An Impact Study', op. cit.

[56] Between 1951 and 1961 the number of New Commonwealth immigrants in London rose from 256,000 to 541,000. See M. Anwar, *The Myth of Return*, London, Heinemann, 1979, p. 4.

[57] See Gardner, op.cit., pp. 39-48.

[58] J. Eade et al. in C. Peach, op.cit., pp. 150-60.

[59] The Decennial Census for 1991 revealed that there were 36,000 Bangladeshis living in Spitalfields, this represents between 60.7 per cent (Decennial Census) and 95 per cent (City Challenge), of the community. It should also be noted that there is undoubtedly a considerable number of illegal immigrants plus those there legally but unwilling to reveal themselves on the Census because of the Poll Tax which was then still in operation.

[60] Conversation with M. Goodmaker, Clothing Industries Co-ordinator, City Challenge, 13 March 1996.

[61] For details of organisation amongst the Jewish tailoring workers of east London see A.J. Kershen, op.cit., Chapter 5.

[62] Conversation with Goodmaker 13 March 1996 and with Peter Corbishley, Clothing Industries Association, East London, 18 March 1996.

---

[63] *Living in Bethnal Green: A Survey of Residents in the Bethnal Green City Challenge Area*, issued by LEPU, South Bank University, London, May 1995, p. vii.

[64] A survey carried out in 1986 suggests as few as 10 per cent of females engaged in homework whilst a more recent report from Peter Corbishley says there is evidence of sewing machines in the homes but little evidence of their being used.

[65] Conversation with the Rev. John Webber, 14 June 1996.

[66] The Sylheti term for home.

[67] *Guardian Education*, 10 September 1996.

[68] Figures from Philip Davis, Statistician, Registry, QMW, 16 April 1996.

[69] Information from Rev. John Webber, date as above.

[70] Conversation with the author, 20 June 1996.

[71] Eastern European Jewish villages in the Pale of Settlement.

[72] Records show that up to 50,000 eastern European Jews did return in the years leading to the First World War, some could not endure the harsh conditions in the ghettos of London and the major provincial cities, others were sent back by the Jewish Board of Guardians as they did not fulfil the requirements of settlement.

[73] Estimates vary as to the exact number of eastern European immigrants that settled in London in the years between 1881 and 1914.

[74] In spite of this today at Passover Jews in the diaspora drink a toast to 'next year in Jerusalem' - the promised land.

[75] Weber, op.cit., p. 39.

[76] Quotation from *Arbeiter Fraint*, 19 March 1907 taken from A.J. Kershen, op.cit., p. 113.

[77] Conversation with M. Goodmaker, 13 March 1996.

[78] Conversation with John Webber, 14 June 1996.

[79] N. Machiavelli, *The Prince*, London, Penguin, 1975 ed., p. 50. The italics in the quote are the author's.

# 6 Keeping the Options Open: Bangladeshis in a Global City

*John Eade*

In this chapter I will argue that the little we know about Bangladeshi migration to London suggests a long-established strategy of keeping options open - a strategy which has changed during the last twenty years with the emergence of a permanently settled community of three generations. This argument will be supported by an historical survey of Bangladeshi migration to Britain during the 19th and 20th centuries which will be followed by a more detailed analysis of developments taking place during the post-Second World War period especially in the 1980s and 1990s.

### A brief history of Bangladeshi migration to Britain

Migration from the Bengal delta to London has been intimately bound up with Britain's colonial expansion and trade. 'A small community of Indian seamen' emerged in the London dock area during the 19th century and these temporary migrants probably included men drawn from the Sylhet district in the Bengal delta as well as those from the Punjab and western India.[1] These seamen or *lascars* stayed for short periods while they waited for a ship returning to British India (usually Calcutta) but a few stayed longer and lived with and/or married local white women, thereby joining the ranks of an urban lumpen-proletariat which the authorities viewed with contempt.[2]

The presence of Sylheti *lascars* in the dock areas of the Victorian East End is significant because their successors have come to dominate Bangladeshi settlement not only in London but across the whole country. However, during the 19th century and down to the 1950s Bengalis working in British ocean-going ships were recruited from other districts within the delta as well, i.e. Chittagong, Noakhali and Comilla. Wherever they came from a prime motivation appears to have been an economic one: to earn money to send, or bring back, to the villages from which they travelled. If they remained in London for any period of time most *lascars* stayed near the port so that they could find work in a returning ship. Very few were prepared to venture far from the East End and engage in the hazardous pursuit of a pedlar, for example.

This century's two world wars stimulated the employment of Sylheti and other workers from the Bengal delta in Britain's mercantile fleet. The increased presence of Bengalis and other migrant workers from Britain's imperial possessions in London, Cardiff, Liverpool, South Shields and other ports was the focus of local hostility in the years immediately following the end of the First World War.[3] The first oral accounts from Bengali *lascars* who came here before and during the Second World War suggest an increase not only of those employed on British ships but also in the numbers of sailors who 'jumped ship' and found work in cities across the country.[4] Some of these sailors stayed for long periods of their adult lives in urban neighbourhoods where they founded the rudiments for a distinctive community life through lodging houses, cafes, restaurants and other small businesses as well as the establishment of religious facilities.[5]

The partition of British India in 1947 and the emergence of an independent India and Pakistan disrupted the pattern of recruitment across the Bengal delta to Britain's merchant fleet. Calcutta had been the head quarters of a recruitment network which spread across the delta during British rule but from 1947 the city remained within the truncated state West Bengal in an independent India. Its economic and social ties with its former hinterland in East Pakistan gradually weakened and East Bengalis were obliged to lobby for jobs on ships through labour and welfare organisers operating in both east and west Pakistan as well as in Britain and the International Labour Organisation at Geneva.[6] These jobs were crucially supplemented by employment in Britain's expanding post-war economy as migrant workers were encouraged to urban-industrial centres from colonial and ex-colonial territories. In 1956, for example, the Pakistan government granted one thousand passports to 'distressed seamen', their survivors, or nominated dependents[7] and Pakistani government rules were later relaxed to permit men other than ex-seamen to 'proceed to the UK for employment'.[8]

The first generation of predominantly male migrant workers came here, therefore, during the late 1950s and 1960s. They travelled mainly from Sylhet and from certain localities within that district - the seamen's villages of central Sylhet. It appears that most of these migrants shared the belief of the older generation of *lascars* that their stay would be temporary.[9] However, like migrants from other parts of the Indian sub-continent, the Caribbean, Africa, Cyprus and Hong Kong, the notion of an eventual return became increasingly tenuous with the arrival of wives and dependants during the late 1970s and 1980s. The number of Bangladeshis in Britain grew almost thirty fold between 1961 and 1991 - from an estimated 6,000 in 1961 to approximately 22,000 in 1970, to 64,561 by 1980 and, finally, to 162,835 by the 1991 national census.[10] A second and now a third generation has developed with an accompanying weakening of direct ties with the country of origin and an increasing investment of economic and social resources within Britain. Even so this process does not preclude the maintenance of a lively interest in Bangladeshi affairs and an 'imagined community' which spans national boundaries.[11]

In retrospect it appears that most Bengali migrants to London and other British cities shared, until recently, a strategy of keeping their options open. Jobs could be found on the ocean-going ships during the colonial period and temporary employment in Britain's industries and service sector was available even before the Second World War and during the post-Second World War period of low unemployment and consumer affluence. Money could be saved and sent back to relatives to help their strategy of land investment and escape from indebtedness.[12] Clearly Britain was not the 'promised land' in the sense of permanent settlement. If anything, the ancestral villages from which these workers came were the promised land. Most migrants were bound by a promise (explicit or implicit) to return eventually to their families, although some *lascars* evidently were keen to get away from their villages and engage in high adventure delaying their return even to the grave. For respectable Muslim Sylhetis their district was imbued with the sanctity of the great fourteenth century *pir*, Shah Jalal, and his 360 disciples[13] - a holy land to which one could return after completing the pilgrimage to the centre of Islam (Mecca and Medinah).

**Bangladeshi settlement in Tower Hamlets**

The oral histories already available suggest that the *lascars* looked for jobs not only in London but in other urban centres across the midlands and the north of England as well as in the ports of Cardiff and Glasgow. The *lascars* laid the foundations for the rapid expansion of the Bangladeshi population which took place after 1956, although it is highly unlikely that they foresaw the permanent settlement of Bangladeshis in Britain which was encouraged partly by increasingly stringent British immigration controls from the mid-1960s onwards. Despite the movement of Bangladeshi migrant workers across Britain a striking feature of Bangladeshi settlement was its concentration within the Greater London area and especially within the East London borough of Tower Hamlets. By the 1991 census 53 per cent of the total Bangladeshi population within Britain was located in Greater London and almost half of this London community was to be found in Tower Hamlets.[14] In Tower Hamlets and elsewhere these settlers from the Bengal delta shared a highly segregated existence - the product of the 'combination of recent arrival, young age structure, large and extended families and poor economic situation'.[15] To this list should be added the strong social and cultural ties created through chain migration from the Sylhet countryside.[16]

Tower Hamlets emerged as the political and cultural dynamo of this rapidly expanding British Bengali population. Settlement within the borough was even more concentrated through the rapid growth of Bangladeshi residents within the western wards so that by 1991 Spitalfields and neighbouring wards contained much higher proportions of Bangladeshis that the borough average of 23 per cent.[17] Indeed, by 1991 Bangladeshis constituted 61 per cent of Spitalfields' total population - one of the few wards in the country which contained a majority of 'ethnic minority' inhabitants.

These western wards boast a vigorous 'British Bengali' economic, political and cultural life which has developed since the late 1970s.[18] Clustering around Brick Lane are the shops, travel agencies, cafes, restaurants, garment factories, voluntary organisations and the London Great Mosque which attract Bangladeshis from across the borough and further afield as well as white Londoners and the more adventurous tourists. Although statistically the Bangladeshi residents in Spitalfields and elsewhere can be justifiably described as an 'encapsulated community'[19] due attention should be paid to the imaginative use of resources in the wider political and cultural arena especially by those from the second generation.[20] 'British Bengalis' aged between 20 and 40 are making a far deeper impact on local political, educational and welfare debates, for example, than their relatively small numbers would imply.

We have very limited information about these different generations of Bangladeshi settlers within Britain. To the statistical data collected by the census and local surveys we can add the pioneering accounts from the *lascars* and the first generation of settlers provided by Adams and Choudhury as well as the discussions concerning the varied activities of those within the second generation.[21] These analyses are limited in the range of issues investigated and the localities where they were undertaken. Tower Hamlets, not surprisingly, has attracted the greatest attention. Consequently, the outline below is intended to be suggestive rather than authoritative, an incitement to further, more profound research by (hopefully) a second generation of those investigating the British Bengali presence within this country.

## The promised land? Views from the *lascars*

Caroline Adams' collection of interviews with ten old seamen[22] is more useful for our purpose here than Choudhury's more recent publications[23] because most of her informants were closely involved with Tower Hamlets. The *lascars* are largely intent on recounting their experiences within Britain from the 1920s onwards and they provide a vivid picture of a highly mobile existence.

Nawab Ali was one of the Sylheti *lascars* who left his village before the Second World War for Calcutta. After working in the dry dock for a time, he got a job in 1939 on a British ship through a *serang* (foreman) who came from the same area of Sylhet. On arrival at Cardiff Nawab Ali jumped ship and made his way to a sailors' lodging house on the Commercial Road and began a string of jobs which included the Savoy Hotel, Veeraswamy's (one of the earliest West End Indian restaurants) and a factory in Coventry before he was conscripted to work in naval ships where he remained until the end of the war. After 1945 Nawab Ali returned to Britain where he began a career as a small businessman in Tower Hamlets and elsewhere. He frankly admitted his involvement in gambling and black marketeering in the bleak early years of post-war Britain and his marriage to a white woman to whom he failed to pay maintenance and spent six weeks in prison.

Nawab Ali was also one of the early community activists. He joined the Pakistan Welfare Association which was founded in 1952 as a seaman's welfare office with premises in Christian Street, Tower Hamlets. He took a keen interest in the East Pakistan crisis of 1970-71 and the formation of an independent Bangladesh. This crisis brought together Bengali activists and white political leaders such as the local MP, Peter Shore, in a campaign which used Sylheti networks across London, the midlands and the north of England but emphasised the role of Bengali entrepreneurs like Nawab Ali based in Tower Hamlets. Significantly Nawab Ali supported such non-Bengali community organisations as the local Community Advice Bureau, the Berner Settlement and Dr. Barnardo's Home as well as establishing links with the locally influential and well resourced Toynbee Hall.

In 1966 Nawab Ali returned to Sylhet for the first time since he left as a young man. His marriage with his first (white English) wife was ended as was his involvement with two other white women. He remained in touch with his three sons and one daughter by his first wife but in 1972 he married a young Bengali woman (presumably from Sylhet) with whom he raised another three daughters and a son. By the time Nawab Ali was interviewed by Caroline Adams he was learning to be a machinist in the garment industry after losing heavily in a Stoke Newington restaurant investment but was still hoping to revive his career as a restaurant owner.

Nawab Ali had kept his entrepreneurial and social options open within Britain but had decided against eventually returning to his country of origin. He was still closely connected with his relatives in Sylhet and his remittances had helped his brother to buy 'a great deal of land' ('seventy or eighty acres') but he did not want to live there. The key factor in explaining the differences between life in London and rural Sylhet was an economic one according to Nawab Ali:

> It is true that if you have money you can be comfortable in the [Sylhet] house. But when you go out of the house there is nothing but trouble - people twist things round and round, tell lies, make trouble all the time. They seem like very bad people - if they are bad people...it is because being poor makes people bad. People in this country are not poor - they can afford to be good.[24]

Despite the antagonism among the young people towards British Bengalis he wanted his new family to grow up in Britain because in 'Bangladesh there are no jobs, no factories or anything'.[25]

Further insight into the attitude of this older generation towards their country of origin was provided by Haji Shirajul Islam. He was born in Sylhet during 1912, left for Calcutta around 1934 with his uncle who was a ship's foreman (*serang*). He worked on Indian-based ships for several years before coming to London on one of the better paying British registered ships as a fireman in the engine-room. After working in a tailor's shop and various restaurants across London, Haji Shirajul Islam returned to the ships in 1940. He also found work in London and Oxford restaurants and ran a lodging house. In 1945 he returned home but came back to the catering business in London and married an Englishwoman who had been working in his restaurant. He visited Sylhet several times with his wife who spoke Sylheti and 'liked our people very much'.[26]

After she died Shirajul Islam retired from his London businesses and 'changed everything':

> I never dreamed I would go and live back in Bangladesh, I never dreamed this, but when she died I had nothing to stay for. I don't care where I am really, I never go anywhere, just I look after my little bit of farm, my mind is quiet, I like to keep out of gossiping and politics and all that.[27]

Shirajul Islam moved back to Bangladesh, married a Bengali woman and began another family in Dacca, the capital of Bangladesh, as well as looking after his farm in Sylhet. After 1971 he gave more time to religious observance. He explained, 'my business used to distract me from practising'[28] - and he had performed the pilgrimage to Mecca and Medinah (the *haj*), and Haji Shirajul Islam's religious and charitable commitments were now directed towards his homeland where he had built an orphanage near his local Sylhet town 'to do something for the people'.[29]

Nawab Ali and Shirajul Islam were closely connected with Tower Hamlets and contributed to its vigorous community political culture but they had both moved around the city, across the country and between different nation-states. They appeared to have been eager to exploit opportunitie, not only for material advancement but also for the enhancement of their reputations as concerned, responsible members of their community (at least as they grew to become grey bearded 'elders'). If Britain was in any sense a promised land for these former *lascars* it was primarily by virtue of the economic opportunities it presented and the wider range of associated options compared with home. While the desire to return home may have been sustained over the year through the 'myth of return' the option of going back to Sylhet was not an easy one to complete. Nawab Ali describes the trouble which he and other *Londonis* encountered when visiting their homeland: an experience which Katy Gardner confirms through her research in Sylhet.[30] Haji Shirajul Islam had moved back to his native country but, interestingly, he chose to live most of the time in Dacca even though he maintained his economic and community ties with the locality from which he had originally migrated.

## The promised land? views from the second generation

As the *lascars* grew older in Tower Hamlets so the Bangladeshi population expanded and a community infrastructure rapidly developed. The Bangladeshi community in this one borough was linked to other concentrations across London (Camden, Westminster and Newham, for example) and urban areas elsewhere (Luton, Birmingham, Coventry, Oldham, Bradford, Sunderland, Cardiff and Glasgow). Individuals and families moved back and forth between these localities as wives and dependants arrived from Bangladesh and sought a foothold in such sectors as housing, employment, welfare benefits and education. Keeping options open remained an important strategy but the range of options changed as it became harder and harder to keep visiting Bangladesh and to find adequate resources within Britain's urban centres.

The second generation have played a vital and increasingly important role in representing their community to public agencies which controls the supply of material resources within Tower Hamlets and elsewhere. A significant number of these second generation British Bengalis have entered the political and administrative arenas of Tower Hamlets during the last twenty years and have deeply influenced public discourses concerning the needs of their fellow British Bengalis. Not surprisingly their deliberations have turned to their continuing links with their country of origin as they have explored the diverse meanings of home. Some insight into these reflections can be gained from a small survey undertaken by the Centre for Bangladeshi Studies during 1992 with twenty young men and women from Tower Hamlets in higher education. While the *lascars* contacted by Caroline Adams were not directly engaged in discussions about home in the 1992 survey these twenty, second generation Bengalis were invited to consider the issue of home on several occasions during their interviews.

The most revealing discussions of 'home' were provided by the ten female respondents. In response to the very open question: 'Where would you say that you belonged ?' a most revealing reply came from Justna, one of the young women, who reflected on the changing perceptions associated with growing up:

> I know they say: 'Your home is where your heart is' but I don't know where my heart is so that makes it difficult, you know. My heart used to be in the heart of the East End when I was younger. (I know I keep referring back to my childhood but that's the only way I can compare it and allow for it). So I know I used to say that I could never go back to Bangladesh and live there. Maybe to stay there for a couple of months but never to live there.
>
> When we used to go on holidays in this country like the Lake District or, say, Preston or somewhere like there in the north, I could say: 'No, I could never live here'. But I enjoyed the time we spent there. We used to have good laughs and everything but I could never see myself living in the countryside. I was like a city person - bright lights and big city, you know. The pollution, the noise and everything else: that is me. Now I am getting older sometimes I just think living in the city is too competitive and I just want to break away from that and I could live in the country.... I think anybody could live anywhere...as long as they feel comfortable where they are living.[31]

Justna describes a changing perception of home which is located within Tower Hamlets, London and the British countryside rather than her country of origin. Her emotional attachments to the home in which she grew up - Tower Hamlets and the East End - are fading as she grows up and looks beyond the city (the bright lights, the noise and the pollution!) to an apparently more peaceful British countryside. While she begins her discussion with dismissing the idea of ever returning to Bangladesh for more than a brief visit she later raises the possibility that she and others 'could live anywhere'. Her country of origin, however, would have to be one among many possible places where she could 'feel comfortable'.

Justna and many of the other interviewees described the ways in which their lives had been shaped by the various social identities which we presented to them, i.e. Bangladeshi, Bengali, Bengali-British, English, European, Londoner, East Ender, Cockney, Muslim, man/woman, black and Asian, working/middle class. Afia, for example, provides a very illuminating discussion of how these identities relate to her own experience and behaviour:

> British? Yes, I am a British citizen. It is to do with having certain rights in this country. And I have lived here for so long. I don't think I could live in Bangladesh although I keep on going on about my loyalties and affiliations. I think I would find it very difficult to live there because of the way I would have to adjust my behaviour.
>
> British, certainly. I don't really identify with white British people but I identify with people who are black and British. There are a lot of us now - about three million black British people in this country now and I think it is important to accept that there are people who were born in this country and this is what they know. This is the sum of what they know - their experiences in this country. It is not...nationalistic. I don't feel nationalistic about being British...It is just another aspect of my identity.
>
> I am not English - I am Bengali. Not English because I would be contradicting myself if I said I was English. I am not white. I am not European - I've got no European heritage...I am a Londoner. Definitely a Londoner and definitely an East Ender but not a Cockney...I am a Londoner - I couldn't live anywhere else but London, I think, and I love living in the East End. I think I am like a lot of people who have grown up in the East End or grown up in London. They feel really territorial and clingy. But London is like that, isn't it? People cling to certain geographical areas and geographical areas have a lot of meaning for them like Brick Lane or Spitalfields has for me.[32]

As yet Afia is not prepared to move beyond the world in which she has grown up although she is well aware of London's multi-racial character and Britain's ethnic diversity. She claims the same citizenship rights as other British people but identifies with the country's black residents rather than its white majority. Being British is, therefore, separate from being nationalistic, i.e. in ways which exclude black people like herself. This exclusivism may account for her rejection of the label 'Cockney' given its popular association with local white people. 'East Ender' is acceptable because it describes the place in which she has grown up rather than a social and cultural exclusivism by certain East End residents. At the same time Afia recognises the fierce attachment to particular localities which can accompany such exclusivism and she refers to her own neighbourhood where British Bangladeshis constitute the majority of residents.

In these two interviews 'home' is not associated with an eventual return to the country of origin, Bangladesh. At the same time they are aware of the ways in which their identification with a 'homeland' has been shaped by their upbringing within a British Bengali, East End home. They move between various worlds and homes as Sultana explains:

> The thing is I have lived in two societies really because when I go home...I am back to being Bangladeshi. And because of my family and my relatives I am more in a Bangladeshi environment than a British (one). So I live two lives, if you like.
>
> ...When I go out it is British society. I don't really like the model any western society has to give about women but then again I don't like our Bengali role of women either.... I do like the Muslim role of women because that's what I believe in and I think, from what I have studied about Islam, that it gives women a lot of freedom to be themselves despite the fact that a lot of people think it doesn't.[33]

Yet for other young women Bangladesh remained a place where they might more fully express their identity both in the domestic and public spheres. Salma wanted to return partly because she felt rejected by the majority in this country:

> I belong totally to Bangladesh and if I think I belong half there then there is...something wrong with me mentally because nobody in England would see me as part of their [country]...I want to retain my identity and possibly go back with it.[34]

Some looked beyond the option of returning to Bangladesh to other countries where they would feel more 'at home'. Shafia referred not only to Bangladesh but 'Asia' in general:

> To tell you the truth I am not too fond of Britain. If we were rich we would live in Bangladesh.... I like [British] education...but if I had my way I would rather live in a different country, hopefully in Asia.[35]

For those who identified strongly with Islam 'home' could not only be Bangladesh but a any country where an Islamic state had been established. Jahanara, for example, explains that:

> I do have a tendency for my motherland [Bangladesh]. But I would [also] say...a Muslim country where probably the law of *sharia*[36] is established...*that* country is where I belong more than anywhere else.[37]

The different values which individuals attached to particular identities seemed to determine whether they saw themselves as belonging within this country or somewhere else. Yet while their elders may have seen a choice between staying in Britain or returning to Bangladesh these young, highly educated women detected a wider range of options which could take them to other countries where they might feel more at home. Their educational success probably encouraged them to look further afield and, as yet, their choice of options was not affected by marital responsibilities. They were not 'tied down', and Shahanara was one person who looked forward to a career which might take her anywhere:

> Where do I belong? I don't really know...I don't think I belong anywhere - just where my life takes me. I belong where the course of my life has taken me. In terms of career I might have to go abroad to get a really good job or do what I really want to do. Yes, you belong where you are needed, where you are appreciated and well paid![38]

This unsentimental attitude towards place was shared by Mujib, one of the male respondents, who explained the categories of 'British', 'Londoner', 'East Ender' and 'Bangladeshi' in the following terms:

> 'British' just means location - where I am. And 'Londoner' basically is also a place. The 'East End' is a place. It is just sort of describing where you are from - what part of the world. I don't think it would be any different if I was somewhere else in the world...I sort of go

> anywhere and I suppose if I went to...[the] States and lived there I would be a New Yorker or whatever. It doesn't really mean anything to me.[39]

**More community, more options**

These individual narratives of living within Britain and maintaining ties with Bangladesh do not provide a uniform and unambiguous interpretation. The picture here confirms Katy Gardner's richer ethnographic analyses which vividly describe the socio-economic processes within rural Sylhet which have shaped the attitudes and activities of *Londonis* in Tower Hamlets and elsewhere within Britain. However, what I want to take further here is her emphasis on the entrepreneurial strategies of Syhleti migrants and their descendants. Working within the structural constraints of limited job opportunities, poor housing, racial discrimination and educational disadvantage it appears that British Bengalis have sought to improve the socio-economic fortunes of their families in Bangladesh and, increasingly, to invest in their community within Britain. Entrepreneurship in this context, therefore, entails not only economic activity but also energies expended within social, cultural and political arenas. Furthermore, these energies extend well beyond the construction and maintenance of ethnic boundaries through community organisations, family and kinship networks, mosques and madrassahs. They entail engagement with mainstream British society of varying degrees of intensity.

As a result of the developments outlined above the emergence of an ethnic community structure does not necessarily entail the restriction or termination of the strategy of keeping options open which was pursued by the *lascars* interviewed by Caroline Adams. Yet the directions in which this strategy can lead have changed with the emergence of three generations of Bangladeshi settlers in London. The placing of 'home' has become more complicated as the relationship with the country of origin has been transformed.

However, the increasing complication cannot be understand solely in terms of Britain and Bangladesh. The explorations of belonging and identity by the highly educated British Bengalis from the second generation must be located within the wider context of national and global developments. During the 1980s and 1990s a pervasive concern with issues of identity has been communicated through the mass media and political debates concerning, for example, the changing features of national political, cultural and social institutions within Europe. Immigration and ethnic minorities are prominent themes within these debates which look beyond Britain and Continental Europe to what is happening across the globe. Attempts to explain the changing economic and political fortunes of particular areas of the globe (for instance, the Pacific Rim, East Asia, America and Africa) explicitly or implicitly acknowledge the ways in which these regions are globally connected. Socially the effect of the global flows of information, images, goods, capital and people is to heighten individual reflexivity about the groups through which identities can be constructed and sustained.[40] New social categories may emerge from a contradictory process which can produce strategies of cultural exclusion as in the discourses of 'New Racism' within Britain during the 1980s as well as hybrid, discontinuous cultural practices.[41]

In what Albrow has boldly described as a 'global age'[42] the issue of a 'promised land' for any individual becomes extremely complicated. In the context of British Bengalis the concept of a promised land raises the issue of location as we have already seen. While Katy Gardner explores the sacred and secular links between Sylhet and Britain's urban centres (*desh* and *bidesh*[43]) the interviews with the university students quoted above suggest a changing vision of 'home' where Sylhet may no longer be the ultimate point of (physical or imaginary) return. Home in the sense of a 'promised land' may be anywhere in Bangladesh or the Middle East where Sylhetis migrants are also found.[44] For some individuals it could be in any country which observes *sharia,* while for others it may be the English countryside, the USA, 'Asia' or wherever, 'as long as they feel comfortable'.

Admittedly the evidence presented to sustain my argument is slender and I have taken care to propose it with caution. However, one of the most striking features of the university students' reactions is the forceful and imaginative way in which the female students articulated their views concerning belonging and identity. Notions of the promised land were traditionally elaborated by men in Jewish contexts, for example. Moreover, Sylheti migration to Britain was initially undertaken by young adult males. Wives and dependants followed later and were widely seen by white people as subservient to their menfolk. Yet in these interviews we see certain young women at least proclaiming their willingness to cross social and cultural boundaries at local and more global levels. Although outsiders might assume that the elaboration of a British Bengali community structure would constrain female members, the interviews reveal individuals asserting their right to keep their options open along a broader front than the ones envisaged by their male elders.

The evidence that a strategy of keeping options open has existed across several generations among Bangladeshis in Britain accords with what we know about the *Londoni* families in Sylhet and their links with the UK from Katy Gardner's pioneering research. Nevertheless I do not want to imply that British Bengalis *as a community* share this strategy. One cannot extrapolate from individual interviews a consensus uniting a particular ethnic minority group. Indeed, the very concept of British Bengalis as an ethnic group rooted in certain social and cultural practices is unsustainable as a description of social 'reality' even though the concept is powerful as a political and ideological construct.[45] Furthermore, I am not claiming that the strategy is part of some inevitable and unilinear process of social and cultural change. Global connectedness, for example, does not in itself result in increased cultural homogeneity around the world.[46] Local reactions to global flows of people, images and goods may result in various revivalisms and fundamentalist movements which seek to resist those flows.[47] Among British Bengalis, therefore, we could discuss the changing discourses concerning Islam and critiques of 'western secular' society.[48]

The diversity of strategic choices which is available to individuals demonstrates the dynamic plurality of social categories and affiliations which is belied by simplistic references to ethnic minority groups such as the Bangladeshi or British Bengali *community*. Although British Bengalis in Tower Hamlets and elsewhere have to operate within certain social, economic and political constraints they are able also to pursue various strategic choices in their everyday lives.

In this chapter we have explored a long-standing strategy which certain individuals have implemented over sixty years and more within Britain. The creation of a diverse community organisational structure during the last twenty years has not prevented younger British Bengalis from adapting the strategy to accommodate changing circumstances. While their elders kept their options open in the context of returning 'home' to Bangladesh these younger men and women look more widely to 'homes' which could be anywhere even if they, not surprisingly, still emphasise certain locations within Britain and further afield.

What does this changing strategy of keeping options open tell us about British Bengali attitudes towards a promised land? The *lascars* interviewed by Caroline Adams saw Britain as a promised land in terms of economic opportunity and material advancement. Spiritually and emotionally the 'promised land' remained their country of origin and, for most, a Sylhet countryside imbued with the sacred heritage of Shah Jalal and his disciples. For the university students from the second generation the 'promised land' was more elusive. Materially it could be located within Britain or other western countries but given their educational attainments they could also return to Bangladesh. Emotionally and spiritually the choices involved in locating the promised land were equally diverse. Some looked again to Bangladesh and others believed that it could be found in the Middle East or any country which observed Islamic law (*sharia*). Some were not sure where to locate it while others did not care.

So we are left with a diversity of opinion which raises some tantalising questions for further research. What little we do know, however, points to a flexible strategy combined with a contemporary reflexivity which indicates, for certain individuals at least, an engagement with processes that transcend the confines of locality (Tower Hamlets) and structural organisation. We now need to discover who else is engaged in these imaginative journeys and whether they are leading in other directions.

**Notes**

---

1 See R. Visram, 'South Asians in London' in N. Merriman (editor), *The Peopling of London: Fifteen Years of Settlement from Overseas*, London, Museum of London, 1993, p. 170; K. Gardner and A. Shukur, '"I'm Bengali, I'm Asian and I'm living here": the changing identity of British Bengalis' in R. Ballard (editor), *Desh Pardesh: The South Asian Presence in Britain*, London, Hurst and Co., 1994, pp. 146-7; K. Gardner, *Global Migrants: Local Lives: Travel and Transformation in Rural Bangladesh*, Oxford, Clarendon, 1995, pp. 39-42.

2 Visram, op. cit., p. 171.

3 Ibid.

4 See C. Adams, *Across Seven Seas and Thirteen Rivers: Life Stories of Pioneer Sylhetti Settlers in Britain*, London, THAP Books, 1987 and Y.

Choudhury, *The Roots and Tales of the Bangladeshi Settlers*, Birmingham, Sylhet Social History Group, 1993, pp. 70-1.

[5] See Adams, op. cit., pp. 39-54 and Choudhury, op. cit., Chs. 2-5.

[6] Adams, op. cit., p. 61-3.

[7] Ibid., p. 62.

[8] Ibid.

[9] See Gardner and Shukur, op. cit., p. 152.

[10] See J. Eade, T. Vamplew and C. Peach, 'The Bangladeshis: the encapsulated community' in C. Peach (editor), *Ethnicity in the 1991 Census*, Vol. 2, London, HMSO, 1996, p. 150.

[11] See J. Eade, 'Reconstructing places: changing images of locality in Docklands and Spitalfields' in J. Eade (editor), *Living the Global City: Globalization as Local Process*, London, Routledge, 1997, pp. 138-45 and Gardner and Shukur, op. cit., pp. 158-60.

[12] Gardner, 1995, op. cit., pp. 66-72.

[13] Ibid., pp. 76-7. A *pir* is a Muslim saint or holy man.

[14] Eade, Vamplew and Peach, op. cit., pp. 157-8.

[15] Ibid., p. 158.

[16] Gardner and Shukur, op. cit., pp. 147-8.

[17] Eade, 1997, op. cit., p. 139.

[18] J. Eade, *The Politics of Community: The Bangladeshi Community in East London*, Aldershot, Avebury, 1989.

[19] Eade, Vamplew and Peach, op. cit.

[20] See J. Eade, 1989, op. cit. and 'Nationalism and the quest for authenticity: the Bangladeshis in Tower Hamlets', *New Community*, 16 (4), pp. 493-503 and 'The political construction of class and community: Bangladeshi political leadership in Tower Hamlets, East London' in P. Werbner and M. Anwar (editors), *Black and Ethnic Leaderships in Britain: The Cultural Dimensions of Political Action*, London and New York, Routledge, pp. 84-107 and Gardner and Shukur, op. cit.

[21] S. Carey and A. Shukur, 'A profile of the Bangladeshi community in London', *New Community*, 12 (3), pp. 405-17; Eade, 1989, op. cit., 1990, op. cit. and 'Quests for belonging' in A.X. Cambridge and S. Feuchtwang (editors), *Where You Belong: Government and Black Culture*, Aldershot, Avebury, 1992, pp. 33-49; Gardner and Shukur, op. cit.; M. Keith, 'Making the street visible: placing racial violence in context', *New Community*, 21 (4), pp. 551-65.

[22] C. Adams, op.cit.

[23] Y. Choudhury, *Roots and Tales,* op.cit. and *Sons of the Empire*, Birmingham, Sylhet Social History Group, 1995.
[24] Adams, op. cit., pp. 93-4.
[25] Ibid., p. 94.
[26] Ibid., p. 106.
[27] Ibid.
[28] Ibid., p. 107.
[29] Ibid.
[30] K. Gardner, 'Migration and rural context in Sylhet', *New Community*, 18 (4), 1992, pp. 579-90; 'Desh, bidesh: Sylheti images of home and away', *Man*, 28 (1), 1993, pp. 1-15, 'Mullahs, miracles and migration: travel and transformation in rural Bangladesh', *Contributions to Indian Sociology*, ns 27 (2), 1993, pp. 213-35 and *Global Migrants, Local Lives: Travel and Transformation in Rural Bangladesh*, Oxford, Clarendon Press, 1995.
[31] Part of this interview was quoted in J. Eade, 'Identity, nation and religion: educated young Bangladeshi Muslims in London's "East End"', *International Sociology*, 9 (3), 1994, p. 390-1.
[32] Part of this interview was quoted in Centre for Bangladeshi Studies, *Routes and Beyond: Voices from Educationally Successful Bangladeshis*, London, Roehampton Institute and Queen Mary College, 1993.
[33] Centre for Bangladeshi Studies, op. cit., p. 33.
[34] Ibid., p. 25.
[35] Original transcript.
[36] *Sharia*: Islamic law.
[37] Centre for Bangladeshi Studies, op. cit., p. 25.
[38] Original transcript.
[39] J. Eade, 'Reconstructing places: changing images of locality in Docklands and Spitalfields' in J. Eade (editor), *Living the Global City: Globalization as Local Process*, London and New York, Routledge, 1997, p. 142.
[40] See U. Beck, A. Giddens and S. Lash, *Reflexive Modernization: Politics, Tradition and Aesthetics in the Modern Social Order*, Cambridge and Oxford, Polity Press and Blackwell Publishers, 1994 and M. Albrow, *The Global Age: State and Society Beyond Modernity*, Cambridge and Oxford, Polity Press and Blackwell Publishers, 1996.
[41] P. Gilroy, *The Black Atlantic: Modernity and Double Consciousness*, London and New York, Verso, 1993; *Small Acts: Thoughts on the*

*Politics of Black Cultures*, London, Serpent's Tail, 1993; S. Hall, 'Political mobilization and identity' in T. Ranger, Y. Samad and O. Stuart (eds), *Culture, Identity and Politics*, Aldershot, Avebury, 1996, pp. 129-35.

42 Albrow, 1996, op. cit.

43 *Desh*: country or home; *bidesh*: a foreign country.

44 K. Gardner, *Global Migrants,* op.cit., pp. 50-2.

45 J. Eade, *The Politics of Community: The Bangladeshi Community in East London*, Aldershot, Avebury, 1989, 'Nationalism and the quest for authenticity: the Bangladeshis in Tower Hamlets', *New Community*, 16 (4), 1990, pp. 493-503, 'Ethnicity and the politics of cultural difference' in Ranger, Samad and Stuart, op. cit., pp. 57-66.

46 A. Appadurai, 'Disjuncture and difference in a global cultural economy' in M. Featherstone (editor), *Global Culture: Nationalism, Globalization and Modernity*, London, Sage, 1990, pp. 295-310.

47 S. Hall, 'The question of cultural identity' in S. Hall, D. Held and A. McGrew (editors), *Modernity and Its Futures*, Cambridge and Milton Keynes, Polity Press and Open University Press, pp. 273-325.

48 K. Gardner and A. Shukur, '"I'm Bengali, I'm Asian and I'm living here": the changing identity of British Benglalis' in R. Ballard (editor), *Desh Pardesh: The South Asian Presence in Britain*, London, Hurst and Co., 1994, pp. 142-64 and J. Eade, 'Quests for belonging' in A.X. Cambridge and S. Feuchtwang (editors), *Where You Belong: Government and Black Culture*, Aldershot, Avebury, 1992, pp. 33-49.

# 7 The Caribbean Diaspora in the Promised Land

*Philip Nanton*

This chapter shifts the focus of attention from 'London' to the notion of the 'promised land'.[1] A case study of the objective material circumstances of the Caribbean community is presented through an analysis of state/community relations. These conditions are used to discuss whether or not the Caribbean community in Britain, 58 per cent of whom live in London, can legitimately be referred to as a 'diasporic community'. Secondly, the evidence provided below enables some speculation on the extent to which this community has encountered 'the promised land'.

The terms 'diaspora' or 'diasporic community' usually refer to exiled victims who have been forcibly ejected from a society, though Cohen has illustrated that it can legitimately be widened to encompass those who leave a society for economic betterment, trading communities, those with a consciousness of their difference from the majority community in a society, those who hold an idea of a return to a promised land or, more generally, those with a sense of their own cultural distinctiveness.[2]

In the past, analysis of state/community relations, particularly those which focus on the United Kingdom population of Caribbean origin,[3] have often examined the strategies of nation-state rejection or hegemony. Alternatively, they have assessed the attempts by the community to overcome, restrict, or in some way cope with, such pressures.[4] As this community has put down roots and further generations have grown in Britain, the notion of this population as 'immigrant' or 'migrant' has become less apposite as a description. By 1990, 57 percent of the officially designated 'Afro-Caribbean' population was registered as born in the British Isles.

Recent analyses have suggested that the community represents a type of 'Caribbean diaspora'. They emphasise a variety of aspects to the population's adaptability. Cohen argues that 'like many Chinese in the Pacific Basin; Australia and the US, and like the East African Asians, the Caribbean peoples in Europe are "re-migrants", "twice migrants"; or a "diaspora of a diaspora"'.[5] Hall suggests they exhibit 'an identity which lives through not despite, difference, by hybridity'. He argues further that 'Diaspora identities are those which are constantly reproducing themselves anew, through transformation and difference'.[6] Gilroy also disentangles the notion of diaspora from its association with kinship and territory and sees in the notion a means of describing a creative syncretic culture which he characterises as the 'Black Atlantic'.[7] James rejects the notion of hybridity and emphasises the population's cohesiveness and common awareness of its position in British society. He claims that 'Caribbean people have sharpened their perspective of their place in the world and jettisoned inter-island rivalry and competition between different shades of blackness and whiteness.' They have discarded 'some of the most absurd and deluding idiocies of Caribbean life' and this places the population in 'a better position to identify with the oppressed within and outside of Britain'.[8]

In this chapter my aim is to provide a case study which highlights particular social and material features of the United Kingdom Caribbean population. These features are inconvenient for the notion of the existence of a Caribbean diaspora presented above and they challenge the legitimacy of applying the term 'diaspora' to the Caribbean origin population in Britain. They also raise considerable doubts about the application of the notion of London as the promised land for the majority of the Caribbean origin population The recognition of this population by the above authors as an expression of a dynamic and adaptive form of social organisation is however of particular value. It helps to overcome static assumptions of cultural essentialism which pervades much of the policy literature about this community. My contention is, however, that ultimately their analyses stray too far from the more prosaic material experience of the people they describe. Two oversights are important.

Firstly, they tend to ignore the implication of the voluntary nature of Caribbean migration and they underestimate the importance of return as a part of the process of migration. Secondly, they underestimate the extent of the population's dependency on the state, both at the level of the individual and, at the level of voluntary and community organisations. The involvement with the state at the level of local government and central government combine to create a higher degree of dependence and incorporation to Britain and Europe than these analysts of the Caribbean diaspora are prepared to recognise.

The chapter examines each of these features in turn. I first examine the issue of migration and in particular return migration. This is followed by key illustrations of the extent of involvement with the state. Involvement with the state is examined first in terms of individuals and organisations then from the perspective of state policies. I discuss the implications of these oversights for the notion of 'diaspora' as applied to the Caribbean origin population and the extent to which this community can be said to have found 'the promised land'.

## Migration and return migration

The presence of the Caribbean origin population in Britain owes much to Britain's long involvement with the region from its days of plunder, mass Carib expulsion and British settlement, to its exercise of imperial and colonial rule over substantial parts of the region. Britain dominated and suppressed island societies to the extent that, as soon as travel was possible, for those with limited economic opportunities, emigration became an important focus.

Among the patterns of Caribbean migration, post World War Two migration to Britain, however, has been relatively small scale - approximately half a million[9] - in comparison with the United States of America, where the various Caribbean communities comprise a total population of some five million. In Britain, immigration has been particularly skewed to Jamaica. A report published in 1966 estimated that 60 per cent of the Caribbean population came from Jamaica alone. This population exceeded the combined population of those from the other countries of the Caribbean.[10] Primary immigration to Britain effectively ended in the late 1960s and since the mid 1960s population growth has come from natural increases. Between 1973-82 net migration from the Caribbean to the UK totalled only 1,800. This was a negligible number compared to the 1950s and compared to the estimated West Indian/Guyanese origin population in Britain which by 1991 totalled 490,000 (see Table 1).

Migration from the West Indies in this post-war period was in no way a forced victim-based expulsion, either at group or individual levels. Peach has demonstrated that net immigration from the West Indies for the years 1955-1966 was highly and significantly inversely related to unemployment rates in Britain.[11] Thus, if there is any pressure to be identified it is located

**Table 1: Population composition of Great Britain by ethnic group**

| | thousands | percentage of population | percentage of all ethnic minorities |
|---|---|---|---|
| Black | | | |
| - Caribbean | 490 | 0.9 | 16 |
| - African | 220 | 0.4 | 7 |
| - Other | 160 | 0.3 | 5 |
| Indian | 820 | 1.5 | 27 |
| Pakistani | 490 | 0.9 | 16 |
| Bangladeshi | 160 | 0.3 | 5 |
| Chinese | 160 | 0.3 | 5 |
| Other | | | |
| - Asian | 220 | 0.4 | 7 |
| - Other | 270 | 0.5 | 9 |
| All minority ethnic groups | 3,020 | 5.5 | 100 |
| White | 51,870 | 94.5 | |

Source: 1991 Census: Ethnic Minorities in Great Britain.

in the demand for labour in the industrial world as well as the rapid decline in rural work opportunities in the Caribbean. Indeed, for a while the government of Jamaica was not particularly enthused by the migration. As is well known, this generation of Caribbean migrants came from rural backgrounds of restricted opportunity where underemployment was high, work was often seasonal and wages low. There was little selection in terms of skills or qualifications during the period of maximum migration between 1955 and 1962.[12] Direct recruitment of workers by British employers did play a small, if significant, part in encouraging migration, but the majority of migrants to Britain, unlike the Francophone DOM experiences, were not directly recruited. They lacked educational opportunity, and on arrival were given, for the most part, a cold and indifferent welcome.

As Peach shows, the early Caribbean experience of work opportunities in Britain bears a striking resemblance to that of the Irish migrant population. That is, the community provided a replacement workforce for native white British people, many of whom experienced some upward social mobility in the 1950s and 1960s. The community did include a significant proportion of skilled men and qualified women, such as nurses, who tended to be employed either in large scale public sector organisations (e.g. transport and the health services) or in traditional industries. Thus, if we include some of the recruiters who went to Barbados to recruit labour, for example the Post Office and London Transport, it is apparent that, from the earliest stage, the involvement of this community with the state sector can be discerned. As Peach notes 'it was the flagging social services and the weaker parts of the industrial economy which used migrant labour as a prop'.[13]

Admittedly, one could argue that the movement to Britain in the late 1940s, 1950s and early 1960s was impelled by notions of economic advancement, misguided assumptions of a return to the mother country and other ideological baggage which many years of British colonial rule undoubtedly encouraged. However, the important point here is the voluntary nature of the population movement to Britain.

By 1987, researchers of the now elderly first generation of the population began to identify a desire to return 'home', expressed both as a longing and a real aspiration.[14] Bhalla and Blakemore[15] surveying this population in Birmingham, also note that compared to older Asian populations, the Afro-Caribbeans were more dissatisfied with British life and showed more signs of wishing to live in another country. Peach, comparing census totals of people born in the Caribbean over the past three decades, argues that return migration had become a growing phenomena. By comparing the 1966 total of the Caribbean born population (330,000) with a 1986-88 total of 233,000, he suggests a decrease of about 97,000 over a twenty-two year period, or a loss of 4,400 per year.[16]

There is considerable evidence that a substantial number of these people have returned to the Caribbean to work or to retire.[17] In 1995, Byron and Condon estimated that around one-tenth of the Caribbean migrants to the UK had already returned to their birth places and that up to one-third may be expected to return to the island where they were born.[18] The evidence of return is also supported by the increasing number of UK pensions paid into Caribbean countries by the UK government. The total number of UK pensions paid in the Caribbean in 1982 was 8,903. By 1988, the number had increased to 16,539.[19] By 1995 the number of UK pensions paid into Jamaica alone amounted to 19,088.[20] Thus, a variety of evidence suggests that the return to the Caribbean from the UK has been ongoing for some time; the process affects a wide cross section of population, is not insubstantial and continues apace.

Thomas-Hope has identified in return migration an integral component of the Caribbean migration circuit.[21] It represents a final step towards a goal which was stated by many arrivants when they landed in Britain in the 1950s. Thus, if there was any exile here, it can be identified for the returners as voluntary and temporary, if perhaps a little longer than was intended. At the same time migrants from the UK are also perceived by those in the societies to which they return as either wealthy, or mad, or both. Many of those returnees become caught up in a dilemma about identity and loyalty. The concept of the promised land becomes double-edged, offering opportunity, at a cost.

At the same time, however, a loosening of the commitment to 'back home', a form of closing of accounts by those in the UK can also be identified. This appears to have taken the forms of declining remittances and an increasing number of permanent unions with white women. Rubenstein has noted in his analysis of return migration that migrants continue to send home remittances for as long as they intend to return.[22] Although the available figures for remittances are not conclusively reliable because of the variety of ways funds may be repatriated, evidence from the Jamaica National Bank suggests that remittances had declined substantially, from \$20,1m (US) in 1975 to \$13m (US) by 1983.[23]

Secondly, official inter-censal estimates indicate a considerably higher percentage of intermarriage between younger males of West Indian descent and White females, compared with inter marriage between older males of West Indian descent and White females. The level of intermarriage between West Indian male heads of households born outside the UK and White women averaged only 15 per cent for the years 1985-1988. For the same years, however, 40 per cent of West Indian origin husbands born in the UK have married White wives (Table 2).

Thus for some, predominantly the second and subsequent generations, there appears to be a *prima facie* case to suggest that some of the Caribbean origin population is not 'reproducing itself anew' but is dividing in a variety of ways. Some form of choice is being made and the need for a tangible association with the Caribbean is beginning to cool. The contrast between a physical return of some, alongside the cooling of a financial and emotional commitment by others, hints at a parting of the ways on one hand and raises the question; what is the nature of the relationship with the promised land for those who remain?

**Table 2: Marriage partners of White and West Indian male heads of household (hoh) by birthplace, 1985-1988**

| | All hoh, % married to white women | hoh born outside UK, % married to white women | hoh born in UK, % married to white women |
|---|---|---|---|
| White | 99.58 | 98.96 | 99.61 |
| West Indian | 17.77 | 15.00 | 40.30 |

Source: Unpublished Labour Force Survey 1981-1988.

## Community dependence and state strategies

The most important but underestimated feature which challenges the legitimacy of the notion of the diaspora in this context is the extent of linkages and, ultimately, the dependence which the Caribbean community exhibits towards the state in Britain. This dependence is clearly a variable one which affects certain sectors of the community more than others. The elements of the community which it appears are most affected are large proportions of the female workforce; the substantial numbers of households who live in and rent public sector housing from local government; individuals in their search for work; and those involved as clients or providers of community organisations established and run by this community. I will examine each of these consecutively.

The 1991 Census estimates that Black-Caribbean women comprise just over one-half (51 per cent) of the Black-Caribbean population. In 1990, an estimated 22 per cent of Afro-Caribbean women were in employment in hospitals or other forms of medical care institutions. This represented the single highest area of female employment for this community, well beyond any other individual demand employment category (See Table 3). Of all women in employment, 77.2 per cent of Afro-Caribbean women work full time.[24] This pattern of employment is essential for the economic survival of families.[25] With a proportion of lone parent, predominantly female-led, households comprising 16.4 per cent of all Black Caribbean households, Brown[26] and Breugel's[27] evidence suggest that 'West Indian' lone parents are less likely to be in employment and are more dependent on benefits. Thus the public sector as employer and welfare agent remains the lynch-pin of institutional support for the female population of Caribbean origin.

Another source of essential support, though grudgingly provided by the state, and at times in the poorest of condition, has been the provision by local government of rented accommodation in substantial quantities on urban housing estates. Much of the debate about this housing in the past has focused on its poor standards, inadequate amenities and discriminatory practices. However the level of provision has remained substantial. For example, for the period 1984-86 an estimated 47 per cent of Afro-Caribbean households rented accommodation from local government. By 1990, despite central government policy changes and attempts to encourage home ownership, this proportion had declined to only 41 per cent. This population has remained the highest single ethnic minority group in the UK in this form of housing tenure.

Economic historians have noted for some time that the British economy has faced long term economic decline since the turn of the century. At times this decline has been particularly acute, reinforced by periodic attempts to restructure labour and capital, with major shifts occurring away from traditional heavy manufacturing industry towards service, high tech industrial development and financial capital exports for higher return overseas. As the home economy contracted and reorganised the impact of unemployment, combined with radical competitive practices, was sharply felt, impacting particularly harshly on the Caribbean origin community. These changes were forceful because of the population's low levels of skill development, its experience of discrimination in employment and its relatively weak educational attainment levels all of which restrict the adaptability for training. The result has been that during the depression of the 1980s and into the 1990s severe unemployment has been the lot for 14 per cent of the total Afro-Caribbean labour force, a factor which is most evident in the 1991 decennial census. This was at a level which was more

**Table 3: Industry distribution by ethnic group, all female employees, 1988-90**

| | All origins | White | Total ethnic minority | Afro-Caribbean |
|---|---|---|---|---|
| | % | % | % | % |
| 0 **Agriculture, forestry and fishing** | 1 | 1 | 0 | 0 |
| 1 **Energy and water supply** | 1 | 1 | 1 | 1 |
| 2 **Extraction minerals, metal manufacture** | 2 | 2 | 1 | 1 |
| 3 **Metal goods, engineering and vehicles** | 5 | 5 | 7 | 6 |
| Motor vehicles and parts | 0 | 0 | 1 | 0 |
| 4 **Other manufacturing** | 9 | 8 | 12 | 7 |
| Textiles | 1 | 1 | 2 | 0 |
| Clothing and footwear | 2 | 2 | 5 | 3 |
| 5 **Construction** | 2 | 2 | 1 | 1 |
| 6 **Distribution, hotels, catering and repairs** | 25 | 25 | 22 | 14 |
| Retail distribution | 15 | 15 | 12 | 7 |
| Hotels and catering | 7 | 7 | 7 | 5 |
| 7 **Transport and communication** | 3 | 3 | 4 | 4 |
| 8 **Banking and finance, etc.** | 12 | 12 | 12 | 12 |
| Business services | 6 | 6 | 6 | 6 |
| 9 **Other services** | 41 | 41 | 40 | 55 |
| Public administration, defence, etc | 6 | 6 | 6 | 6 |
| Education | 12 | 12 | 6 | 8 |
| Hospitals, medical care institutions | 9 | 8 | 15 | 22 |

Source: 1988, 1989, 1990 Labour Force Surveys (GB).

| African Asian | Indian | Pakistani | Bangladeshi | Chinese | African | Other/ mixed |
|---|---|---|---|---|---|---|
| % | % | % | % | % | % | % |
| 0 | 0 | 1 | * | 0 | 0 | 0 |
| 2 | 0 | 0 | * | 0 | 0 | 0 |
| 2 | 1 | 1* | 1 | 2 | 1 | 0 |
| 11 | 8 | 9 | * | 1 | 2 | 1 |
| 1 | 2 | 1 | * | 0 | 0 | 0 |
| 14 | 22 | 33 | * | 4 | 4 | 6 |
| 4 | 5 | 4 | * | 0 | 0 | 1 |
| 4 | 9 | 22 | * | 2 | 3 | 1 |
| 0 | 0 | 0 | * | 0 | 1 | 2 |
| 24 | 22 | 33 | * | 41 | 20 | 25 |
| 18 | 14 | 23 | * | 7 | 8 | 14 |
| 1 | 5 | 7 | * | 33 | 10 | 7 |
| 8 | 4 | 0 | * | 4 | 2 | 4 |
| 17 | 13 | 4 | * | 10 | 11 | 12 |
| 5 | 7 | 1 | * | 5 | 6 | 6 |
| 21 | 28 | 20 | * | 39 | 53 | 44 |
| 7 | 5 | 6 | * | 3 | 10 | 8 |
| 4 | 5 | 4 | * | 5 | 7 | 7 |
| 6 | 9 | 3 | * | 19 | 22 | 15 |

* Sample size too small

than twice the unemployment of the White population (Table 4). But for the sub grouping of the younger males aged 16-24, the level of unemployment was even higher, estimated in the 1991 Census to be 37.6 per cent (Table 5). In turn, these levels of unemployment have exacerbated public sector dependency. Thus, those seeking employment had little option but to seek welfare, search for work in public sector-operated job centres or attempt to take up opportunities for retraining through various public programmes. With very low rates of self-employment for this group - in 1991, they stood as low as 6.7 per cent - the options for any alternative strategies were closed.

**Table 4: Unemployment rates by ethnic group, age and sex, 1988-90**

| | **Age 16-24** | | | **Age 25-44** | | | **Age 45-64** | | |
|---|---|---|---|---|---|---|---|---|---|
| | **All** | **M** | **F** | **All** | **M** | **F** | **All** | **M** | **F** |
| All origins | 11 | 12 | 10 | 7 | 6 | 7 | 7 | 7 | 5 |
| White | 10 | 11 | 9 | 7 | 6 | 7 | 6 | 7 | 5 |
| Total ethnic minority | 19 | 20 | 19 | 11 | 11 | 11 | 12 | 13 | 10 |
| Afro-Caribbean | 23 | 24 | 13 | 12 | 11 | 12 | 11 | 15 | 6 |
| African Asian | 12 | 9 | 15 | 7 | 6 | 8 | 13 | 11 | 17 |
| Indian | 16 | 18 | 13 | 10 | 9 | 11 | 11 | 11 | 13 |
| Pakistani | 30 | 31 | 30 | 18 | 18 | 18 | 22 | 21 | * |
| Bangladeshi | 19 | 15 | * | 23 | 26 | * | 33 | 33 | * |
| Chinese | 7 | * | * | 9 | 12 | 4 | 2 | 2 | * |
| African | 27 | 28 | 26 | 10 | 13 | 7 | 11 | 7 | * |
| Other/Mixed | 13 | 14 | 11 | 10 | 8 | 14 | 6 | 5 | 7 |

* Sample size too small

Source: 1988, 1989, 1990 Labour Force Surveys (GB).

**Table 5: Male unemployment by ethnic origin, 1991**

| | All % | Age 16-24 % |
|---|---|---|
| White | 10.7 | 17.4 |
| Black Caribbean | 23.8 | 37.6 |
| Black African | 28.9 | 41.6 |
| Black Other | 25.5 | 35.2 |
| Indian | 13.4 | 23.4 |
| Pakistani | 28.5 | 36.1 |
| Chinese | 10.5 | 15.4 |
| Other Asian | 14.2 | 29.4 |
| Other | 19.7 | 29.4 |

Source: D. Owen, *Ethnic Minorities in Great Britain: Economic Characteristics*, Coventry, Centre for Research in Ethnic Relations, University of Warwick, 1993, tables 6 and 7.

Another, though more unwelcome form of involvement with the state is reflected in the over-representation of the Black Caribbean population as suspects and defendants at all stages of the criminal justice system. In 1993 male prisoners of Caribbean origin comprised seven per cent of all prisoners although the Black-Caribbean population comprised only 0.9 per cent of the total population. Three reasons have been suggested for this over-representation. It has been ascribed to socio-economic causes, discrimination within the criminal justice system and to 'cultural' factors. Whatever the reason, evidence has accumulated also that Blacks are the targets of proactive policing. Once in the criminal justice system the black population are less likely to be filtered out. At the same time antipathy remains high between the Black population and the police. The 1988 British Crime Survey demonstrated that 70 per cent of all Afro-Caribbeans surveyed believed that the police were not even-handed but tended to pick on certain groups.

In these circumstances, whether created by structural change or racism, community-based organisations soon emerged as supportive and partial alternatives to state provision in welfare, homelessness, supplementary schooling and other areas. These organisations provide leadership, ease alienation and attempt to meet particular needs. While often proclaiming the 'self-help' nature of their activities, and oppositional rhetoric against local and central government, in practice they exhibit substantial levels of dependence on local or central government financial support to enable them to carry out their tasks.

It is not possible to estimate accurately how many Afro-Caribbean organisations serve the community. However, in drawing a funding register for central government one estimate identified over 1,547 groups which catered for Black people, of which 488 were run by people of Caribbean origin.[28] Much of the influence of these organisations and many of their activities as community groups and voluntary organisations have developed out of small scale, holistic initiatives.

A sample survey of Afro-Caribbean organisations conducted by Hinds in 1992 among predominantly London based organisations (the area in which 58.2 per cent of the Black-Caribbean population is located) illustrated the extent of this dependence. From 124 organisations surveyed, 44 per cent were totally dependent on local councils for their funding. This proportion increased to 62.2 per cent if part-funding from local councils is included. If central government and other elements of state funding is included then his respondents indicated that 90 per cent of these organisations rely on state funds in some form. As Hinds' study noted: 'This heavy overall dependence on local councils for funding means that the viability of many Caribbean community-based organisations is inextricably linked to the funding policies of local councils'.[29]

## Central and local government racialised policy-making

When the wider effect of national policies are examined two strategies can be discerned which have a direct impact on the Caribbean population. The strategies can be broadly identified as a those of exclusion of new arrivals, and incorporation of those resident in the UK. The former have been shaped by increasingly racialised immigration restrictions, developed since Britain's Immigration Acts of 1962 and 1971, and reinforced by the patriality notions of the Nationality Act 1981. Whereas the chances of a national from Australia or New Zealand being refused entry at a UK port in 1987 were 1:2,360 and 1:1,640 respectively, the chances of a Caribbean national visitor was 1:1,193 for the same year.[30] Restrictions have been developed to the extent that they affected even temporary family reunifications from the Caribbean region. Entry refusals imposed on Jamaican travellers to UK grew from 48 in 1979 to 803 in 1989.

The strategies of incorporation offer individual rights of action in Tribunals against discrimination as well as independent investigation and national agency regulation through the government-sponsored Commission for Racial Equality. At the level of local government intervention, policies have till recently included a mixture of area-focused and racialised programmes, based on notions of deprivation. Many local councils use monitoring techniques to encourage group proportionality to enhance employment structures and test for service relevance. So called 'multi-cultural' policies have at times reinforced notions of fundamental difference overtly, and at others under the disguise of area policies.[31]

Both strategies of exclusion and incorporation reinforce the community's focus inwardly away from the Caribbean and towards Britain and Europe. The policies also contribute to the changes in the nature of the population from individual island focused communities to a metropolitan and urban focused racialised minority group.

**Discussion**

Can a diasporic population exist if significant elements of the population so described are characterised by high levels of state dependence, effective incorporation policies and reliance on relatively developed strategies of protection in the voluntarily chosen country of settlement? Do these experiences suggest the arrival into a promised land? These questions return the reviewer to a problem of definition.

Cohen has usefully demonstrated how the term 'diaspora' is open to wider interpretation than the common association with the tradition of victims and catastrophe involving a forcible dispersal of people and their subsequent unhappiness in their countries of exile. He argues that strategies of organisational adaptability, specialised and effective trading practices as well as annexation of land and the declaration of independent statehood, all legitimately encompass the diasporic experience. The late modern era of globalisation, he further suggests, has enhanced the practical, economical and affective roles of diasporas, showing them to be particularly adaptive forms of social organisation.[32]

The political Right see in diasporas an uncontrollable and dangerous trend which leads ultimately to violence and chaos. This is captured in the

British Conservative politician Enoch Powell's notion of 'the alien wedge' which his 'rivers of blood' speech brought to the surface in 1968. In 1978 Mrs Thatcher linked herself to that view. When she was interviewed about trends in 'New Commonwealth' immigration she stated:

> people are really rather afraid that this country might be swamped by people of a different culture. The British character has done so much for democracy, for law, and done so much throughout the world that if there is any fear that it might be swamped, then people are going to be rather hostile to those coming in.

More recently, Woollacot, writing in the *Guardian,* has argued in general terms that

> deeply urbanised, highly mobile and culturally mixed societies penetrated by intercontinental diasporas of diverse origins breed the alienation, the anonymity, the anger and the attraction to covert and irregular movements that lead to acts of terror. This is a way of life in which new benefits and religions proliferate in the vacuum left by traditional systems and a generalised culture of violence justifies the use of any means that furthers the expression of religious or political identity.[33]

As suggested above, Cohen, Hall, Gilroy and James, who focus on the 'Caribbean diaspora', are more optimistic. Their optimism stems from the community's capacity for adaptation or its cohesive fighting powers arising out of a racialised identity. This discussion however has identified a resounding silence and neglect of important characteristic features of the Caribbean origin population with which the term 'diaspora' is being associated. These features illustrate a population making up its mind about Britain, about staying or going. Both decisions have implications for the notion of 'the promised land'.

If the term 'the promised land' includes a sense of economic fulfilment within a limited time span, then it is arguable that this promise was fulfilled for a small but growing number of relatively well-off pensioners who now live in the Caribbean and draw state pensions. It may be also that this promise was kept for some younger people who have benefited from training in the UK and who have returned to the Caribbean.

For those who have stayed on in the increasing certainty of making Britain their home, the experience for the past thirty years in 'the promised land' is one of contrasts. Optimists can point to increasing social group organisation, integrated patterns of housing, intermarriage and, to a limited extent, some upward occupational class mobility. Pessimists identify very little fulfilment in the on-going close negative and disproportionate associations with the state's custodial and welfare institutions which indicate marginalisation and dependency higher than that experienced by other groups of settlers.

**Notes**

---

[1] Sections of this chapter appeared in P. Nanton, 'The Caribbean Diaspora in Question: The United Kingdom Context' in *International Journal of Comparative Race and Ethnic Studies*, 11 (1), 1995, pp. 42-55.

[2] R. Cohen, 'Rethinking "Babylon": Iconoclastic Conceptions to the Diaspora', *New Community*, 21 (1), 1995, pp. 5-18.

[3] Official statistics have referred to the Caribbean origin population in the United Kingdom variously as 'West Indian/Guyanese', 'Afro-Caribbean' and - the most recent category used in the 1991 Census - 'Black-Caribbean'. I have followed the designated terms when referring to studies cited in the text. For a discussion of some of the implications of the categorisation of ethnic minorities, including the Caribbean origin population in the United Kingdom see P. Nanton, 'Official Statistics and Problems of Inappropriate Ethnic Categorisation', *Policy and Politics*, 20 (4), 1995, pp. 277-85.

[4] W. James and C. Harris (editors), *Inside Babylon: the Caribbean Diaspora in Britain*, London, Verso, 1993.

[5] Cohen, op.cit., p. 22.

[6] S. Hall, 'Cultural Identity and Diaspora' in J. Rutherford (editor), *Identity: Community, Culture, Difference*, London, Lawrence & Wishart, 1990, p. 235.

[7] P. Gilroy, *The Black Atlantic: Modernity and Double Consciousness*, London, Verso, 1993.

[8] W. James and C. Harris, op.cit., pp. 244, 280.

[9] C. Peach, 'The Caribbean in Europe: Contrasting Patterns of Migration and Settlement in Britain, France and the Netherlands', Research Paper No. 15, CRER, University of Warwick, Warwick, 1991.

[10] E.J.B. Rose, N. Deakin, M. Abrams, V. Jackson, M. Preston, A. Vanagi, B. Cohen, J. Gaitskell and P. Ward, *Colour and Citizenship: A Report on British Race Relations*, London, OUP, 1969.

[11] C. Peach, *West Indian Migration to Britain: A Social Geography*, London, OUP for Institute of Race Relations, 1968.

[12] C. Peach, op.cit., 1991, p. 7.

[13] Ibid.

[14] S. Fenton, *Ageing Minorities, Black People as They Grow Old in Britain*, London, CRE, 1986.

[15] A. Bhalla and K. Blakemore, *Elders of the Minority Ethnic Groups*, Birmingham, AFFOR, 1981.

[16] C. Peach, op.cit., 1991, p. 12.

[17] R. Nutter, 'Implications of Return Migration from the United Kingdom for Urban Employment in Kingston, Jamaica', in R. King (editor), *Return Migration and Regional Economic Problems*, London, Croom Helm, 1986.

[18] M. Byron and S. Condon, 'A Comparative Study of Caribbean Migration from Britain and France: Towards a Context-Dependent Explanation', in *Transactions of the Institute of British Geographers* (New Series), Vol. 21, pp. 91-204.

[19] W. James and C. Harris, op.cit.

[20] Department of Social Security, *International Payments of Return Pensions and Widow Benefits Allowance*, Newcastle, 1995.

[21] E.M. Thomas-Hope, 'Return Migration and its Implications for Caribbean Development' in R. Pastor (editor), *Migration and Development in the Caribbean: the Unexplained Connection*, Boulder, Westview, 1985.

[22] H. Rubenstein, 'Return Migration to the English-Speaking Caribbean: Review and Commentary', in W.F. Stinner, K. de Albuquerque and R.S. Lyce-Laporte (editors), *Return Migration and Remittance: Developing a Caribbean Perspective*, Washington DC, 1982.

[23] P.Y. Anderson, 'Migration and Development in Jamaica' in R.A. Pastor, op.cit.

[24] R. Bhavanani, *Black Women in the Labour Market: a Research Review*, Manchester, Equal Opportunities Commission, 1994.
[25] I. Breugel, 'Sex and Race in the Labour Market', in *Feminist Review*, No. 32, Summer, 1989.
[26] C. Brown, *Black and White Britain*, London, Policy Studies Institute, 1984.
[27] Op.cit.
[28] S.V. Small, *From Arts to Welfare: a Bibliography of the Black Voluntary Sector*, London, SIA, 1994, p. 24.
[29] A. Hinds, *Report on Organisations Serving the Afro-Caribbean Community*, London, West Indian Standing Conference, 1992, p. 51.
[30] Joint Council for the Welfare of Immigrants, *Target Caribbean: The Rise in Visitor Refusals from the Caribbean*, London, JCWI, 1990, p. 11.
[31] P. Nanton, 'The New Orthodoxy: Racial Categories and Equal Opportunity Policy', *New Community*, 15, (4), July 1989, pp. 549-64, and P. Nanton and M. Fitzgerald, 'Boundaries or Thresholds? Race Relations Policies in Local Government', in W. Ball and J. Solomos (editors), *Race and Local Politics*, London, Macmillan, 1990.
[32] R. Cohen, op.cit.
[33] M. Woollacot, 'Living in the Age of Terror', *Guardian*, 22 April 1995.

# 8 Living in Bethnal Green: Together or Apart?

*Mike Fenton*

My involvement with Bethnal Green is relatively recent. In 1993, the Local Economy Policy Unit (LEPU) won the contract to carry out the evaluation study of the five year Bethnal Green City Challenge programme. This was the first time that I had worked in the area, although LEPU, and in particular its Director Sam Aaronovitch, has a long and close involvement with the locality. Bethnal Green is an exciting place to work - its sense of history, its contrasts and its people provide a special backdrop. Even the more mundane elements of the study have appeared stimulating in the Bethnal Green context.

Over the last three years of working in Bethnal Green, two questions have constantly recurred. First, if we return in 20 years time what will the area look like and who will be living here? Secondly, are we seeing a coming together of the communities who live in Bethnal Green or is a form of segregated living occurring?

Our evaluation study has not been directly related to these questions but we have collected rich data for other purposes which casts light on these issues. We undertook a residents' survey in 1995[1] which followed on from a survey carried out by SCPR in 1993.[2] Another survey obtained responses from over 1,000 school pupils in Tower Hamlets.[3] We have also undertaken interviews with head teachers, developers and others interested in the future of the area. In addition, we have been charting the changes taking place in the economic and social profile of the area since the beginning of the City Challenge programme in 1992.[4] This chapter describes our findings.

**The moving population**

Most of the information which we present in this chapter relates to the area as defined for the Bethnal Green City Challenge programme. This consists of the Spitalfields ward and parts of the wards of Weavers' and St. Peter's. It has a population of about 15,000, which is about a half of that of the former administrative Bethnal Green Neighbourhood.

The Bethnal Green area is well known for the fact that it has been the first stopping point for people from many different ethnic groups. The best documented waves of immigration have been the Huguenots, the Jews and the Bangladeshis. Other migrants have been the Irish in the 1840s and Maltese and Cypriots after the Second World War. Bethnal Green's proximity to the ports of London and to the City made it an attractive location. The presence of a large volume of poor quality accommodation for rent in the private sector gave people with few financial resources, and no immediate access to public sector housing, the opportunity to move into the area.

Over time, these communities have moved away from the area. In some cases, this was a result of redevelopment and dispersal, but often it has represented the choice patterns of households seeking an improved way of life. In their place came other households with low levels of financial resources and few options. The area therefore retained its image of having a population with poor economic activity, whilst in fact it has been the starting point for much personal advancement.

The area is now predominantly populated by two ethnic groups - Bangladeshis and white British. Between them they comprise over 90 per cent of the population. They have very different household compositions. In our residents' survey we found that over three-quarters of the Bangladeshi households have children under 16 whilst the figure for the white British households is only 18 per cent This has significant implications for the future mobility patterns of the two groups and the social and cultural life of the area.

There is as yet no evidence of other groups moving into the area in large numbers. Some Somalis have moved in and there is a Somali community centre in the area, but on present trends they are likely to remain a small part of the population.

## A changing landscape

The area surrounding Bethnal Green has seen major changes taking place. To the west, the development of the Broadgate site at Liverpool Street station sent a message that the City was eager to move eastward. At the end of the 1980s it was generally assumed that major speculative office development would creep into Spitalfields and would lead to the loss of a significant amount of the existing employment base.

To the east, the development at London Docklands transformed the old port area. In the place of low quality business premises and manual skill jobs has appeared shiny office blocks and highly paid jobs in financial, business and professional service sectors. The number of jobs in Docklands has grown from just over 27,000 in 1981 to 70,000 in 1996. However, most of these jobs have been taken by commuters from all parts of London and beyond. Interestingly, figures from the 1991 Census showed that there were more people working in Docklands who lived in Hounslow in west London than lived in Tower Hamlets. This highlights the difference between job creation and job access. The fact that jobs are created in a particular area does not guarantee that local people will receive any favours in competing for the available work.

The Bethnal Green area itself has been the subject of less dramatic but nonetheless substantial changes. On the employment side, the closing of the Spitalfields Market and the Trumans Brewery led to the loss of many jobs but also created the opportunities for new developments. These have been a long time in arriving but they are now beginning to come on stream. The first commercial development on the Spitalfields Market site will see a Dutch bank, ABN Amro, bring over 1,000 jobs into the area. Private sector housing developments are also planned. The Trumans site has now been sold and it is proposed to create a Textile and Clothing Industry Centre of Excellence and a commercial village complex.

More important though, have been the gradual changes which have taken place in the quality of social rented housing and the increase in the number of units in the owner occupied sector. The unbelievable conditions in which many Bangladeshis have had to live is graphically set out in Charlie Forman's book *Spitalfields: a Battle for Land.*[5] He also describes the long fight which local communities have been engaged in for better living conditions. This has been a battle against the spread of office developments and a struggle for better quality housing and a fairer allocations system.

The battle is far from over but the quality of much of the stock has improved. This has been a result of a number of factors. The improvement works carried out by the local authority housing department, the recent expenditure through the Bethnal Green City Challenge programme into both social housing and owner occupation; the influx of new housing association units and the development of new owner occupied homes.

## Living together or apart?

There are a number of ways that this issue could be considered. People interact in terms of where they live, work, go to school, worship and take their leisure. The information that we have collected largely relates to residential patterns and to issues affecting the schooling of local children. However, it is of interest to note that the employment locations of Bangladeshi and white British residents display markedly different patterns. In our residents' survey, we found that 36 per cent of Bangladeshi respondents in employment worked in Bethnal Green compared to 18 per cent of white British respondents. Interestingly, 22 per cent of British respondents worked in the City compared to only three Bangladeshi interviewees. Many of those who live in Bethnal Green do work in the City but they are not Bangladeshi.

### *Residential patterns*

The residential segregation of ethnic groups is not new. Cities have always had areas where there are concentrations of particular groups and areas where native residents have sought to keep out any newcomers. This is based on a mixture of forces. The lack of purchasing power, combined with discrimination amongst sellers and estate agents have acted as barriers to many ethnic minority households wanting to move into owner occupation. The allocation process in the local authority sector kept many estates whites only. The fear of racial violence acted as a further constraint on the movement of households away from areas where there was relative safety in numbers. Nowadays the more overt forms of discrimination are less pronounced. Most local authority housing departments have introduced ethnic monitoring and would not tolerate the abuses which took place in the 1960s and 1970s. There is an increasing awareness of racial violence on estates and of the need to move the perpetrators not the victims of such violence. Estate agents can no longer accept discriminatory instructions.

As a result, should we expect to see a gradual movement of the Bangladeshi community away from Bethnal Green and into other non-local authority tenures? For this to happen, four elements need to be in place. First, Bangladeshi households must want to move. This will be a mixture of push factors for those who decide that they no longer want to live in Bethnal Green, and pull factors for those who can see a better quality of life in another area. The changes taking place in Bethnal Green may well be altering these perceptions. Secondly, the discriminatory practices which used to flourish and prevented access to housing do need to have disappeared for good. Thirdly, the Bangladeshi community need to believe that they are welcome in different areas. Even if the level of prejudice has declined, if the Bangladeshi community still believe that it is unsafe for them to move to another estate or that they will not be welcome on a new housing development then they will not place themselves in these circumstances. Finally, the Bangladeshi community needs to have the opportunity to move. They need the financial resources if they wish to buy and they need the offers of suitable accommodation in the social housing sector.

It is difficult to unravel these elements. Households with low levels of financial resources have fewer options open to them. The upheaval and costs involved in moving may well be too great especially if they are unsure of what awaits them in a new location. This suggests that the level of mobility will be less than might be expected from an analysis of the overcrowded and sub-standard conditions being endured.

*The desire to move*

Our residents' survey looked in some detail at housing circumstances and respondents' views of Bethnal Green as a place to live. Generally, people told us that they liked living in Bethnal Green. Over four out of five respondents viewed the area as either 'a very good place to live' or 'quite a good place to live'. This figure had increased by over 10 per cent since the 1993 survey. Less than a fifth said that it was 'not a very good place to live'. There was virtually no difference in responses between the Bangladeshi and white British households. We also looked at the issue in another way by asking how respondents thought that Bethnal Green had changed in the last three years. About three-quarters thought that it had improved with little difference between the responses of the two groups.

When we looked at the desire of households to move from Bethnal Green, we find that only one in ten Bangladeshi respondents wanted to move to a different area. Of the relatively small number who did want to move, over half would like to move to another part of Tower Hamlets. Interestingly, amongst young Bangladeshis in the 16-24 age group, the desire to move to a different area only increases marginally to 11 per cent. The evidence suggests that the Bangladeshi community wish at present to remain in Bethnal Green. Most certainly, they want better housing but this is not equated with the view that the only way to improve housing conditions is to leave the area altogether.

*Improving quality*

Forman vividly describes the dreadful conditions in which Bangladeshis were living: 'No hot water, no inside toilet, no bath. With slight variations, this is how many hundreds of Bangladeshi families were living in the 1970s and even the 1980s.'[6] Initially, it was mainly Bangladeshi men living in the private rented sector. They were having to endure extreme overcrowding in accommodation which was often not fit for habitation. Initially, many believed that they would only be living here for a short time before returning home. Once the decision was made to bring the family over to this country then everything needed to change. The size of accommodation which was required increased and families aspired for a much improved quality of home. This was no longer going to be provided in the private rented sector so the focus of attention turned to the local authority stock. This too was found wanting. The condition of the council stock also left much to be desired:

> There were blocks with no lifts, no heating and sometimes no bathrooms. More of the council housing had been built in the bleakest era of the 1960s. The new part of the Chicksand Estate is a prime example. Potentially attractive maisonettes were un-heatable - with bedrooms cantilevered out from the main structure of the building so that they had three outside walls as well as floors and ceilings which were outside surfaces. The houses on the estate had been designed so that the roofs leaked perpetually, and the timber doors and windows were warped and rotted.[7]

In recent years, there have been great efforts to improve the quality of the housing. This has come about through improvements in the existing local authority stock and new building by housing associations and private housebuilders. The impetus for this initially came from the local authority. Between 1981 and 1991, the percentage of households in Spitalfields ward lacking or sharing a bath/shower and/or inside toilet dropped from 14 per cent to three per cent. This percentage was still over twice the figure for Tower Hamlets as a whole. However, much more needs to be done. Preliminary results from a borough wide survey of the local authority stock showed that 'in order to bring the Council's stock into a good state of repair, work is required to nine out of 10 Council homes'.[8]

More recently, the advent of Bethnal Green City Challenge has led to increased investment in the housing stock. The City Challenge output figures show that almost 1,200 local authority properties were improved in the first four years of the programme. This is almost half the number of Council homes in the area. Confirmation of this is provided by Building Control information related to the Bethnal Green Neighbourhood (an area about twice the size of the City Challenge area) which shows that the number of local authority improvements increased from 161 in 1992 to 623 in 1995.

There has clearly been an improvement in the housing conditions of local residents. Overall, nearly half of the respondents in our survey thought their homes were in very good or quite good condition (an increase of five per cent since 1993). This was matched by a decline in the numbers who viewed their homes as poor or very poor (down from 22 per cent to 16 per cent). However, there were great variations in the responses by ethnic group. Bangladeshis were over three times more likely than white British residents to state that their homes were in poor condition (24 per cent as compared to seven per cent). It might be thought that this is related to the different tenure profiles of the two groups, but if we look at households in local authority dwellings, then Bangladeshis are still three times more likely to rate their homes as in poor or very poor condition. Although great improvements have been made, there is still perceived inequality in the quality of accommodation which can be obtained.

In addition, the problem of overcrowding remains and is likely to get worse. Figures from the 1991 Census show that nearly one in three households in the Bethnal Green area of Bangladeshi, Indian or Pakistani origin lived at a density of more than one point five persons per room. This compared to less than one in a hundred white households who were living at this density. Our residents' survey highlighted some extreme examples. Over 40 per cent of the Bangladeshi households consisted of six or more people. Of these, over a quarter lived in one or two bedroom accommodation. Many of these households had young children. As they grow up and become teenagers, the impact of this overcrowding will become even more severe.

*Building for the future?*

The area has also seen significant increases in the number of new housing units built in the area. Over the first four years of the City Challenge programme, over 900 new homes have been built. Well over half have been for owner occupation with the remainder being built by housing associations. As a result, the percentage of the stock which is now in owner occupation is estimated to be 27 per cent with local authority units now making up less than half (45 per cent) of the total. Whilst the figure for owner occupation is low by national standards, it represents a considerable change on the traditional view that the housing in the area is almost totally in Council control.

The housebuilding programme should be providing existing residents with the opportunity to improve their housing condition through the purchase of their own homes. However, there is, as yet, little evidence that Bangladeshi households are taking up this option. Overall, only nine per cent of the Bangladeshi households in our survey were in owner-occupied housing as compared to 32 per cent for the white British group. If we look at the situation of households who have moved into owner occupation in recent years, then we find that they were largely white British households without children. Of 30 households in owner occupation we interviewed which had lived in Bethnal Green for less than five years, 27 were white British and only three of these had children under 16 living in the home. Over 60 per cent of the owner-occupiers had degrees. The new homes for owner occupation are allowing younger well-educated white households to move into the area. Often this is related to the fact that they have a job in the City or nearby. Over a half gave as a reason for moving into the area a desire to be nearer work.

Far from easing the housing problems of Bangladeshi households, the move to encourage owner-occupation may exacerbate the situation. As we can see, in the short term there is no evidence that it is benefitting Bangladeshis. In the longer term it may increase the competition for land and squeeze out moves to build more social housing. In work that we did looking at the investment opportunities in the area, the only sector which was seen to be buoyant was the housing sector and in particular the growing interest in owner occupation. It is quite likely that more private house builders will be attracted to the area and that this will increase land values so making it more difficult for housing associations to compete. With a critical mass of development taking place, the image of the area is beginning to alter. This will itself then create an additional demand to move into the area. The battle for land, as Forman put it, is still there but now it is beginning to move from one with office developers to one with private house-builders.

*Young people's views*

It is a truism to say that the future of the area lies to a large extent in the hands of the young people of the area. Their decisions on whether or not to stay in the area will determine the future community profile. Their actions can affect the whole image of the area and the path of its development. It is therefore of immense interest to look at the aspirations of young people and to analyse what they think about the area and what they are looking for in terms of their future.

To help us understand more about the processes taking place, LEPU carried out a survey of 1,005 secondary school pupils aged 13-18 in Tower Hamlets.[9] Of these, 122 gave addresses which were identified as being in the Bethnal Green City Challenge area. Some of the questions were similar to those we used in the Residents' survey which allowed us to see if young people have a different perception from their parents.

Generally, Bangladeshi youngsters in Tower Hamlets have a lower desire to move out of the area than other groups. About one-third stated that they would like to move out of the borough compared to 60 per cent of the white British sample. Interestingly, only ten per cent of Bangladeshis expressed a wish to live abroad as compared to over a quarter of young white British respondents.

When the young students were asked why they would want to move, there was an emphasis in the answers on obtaining better housing, to feel less crowded, to obtain an improved environment and to escape from crime. Reasons which featured less prominently, were to get a better job, lack of leisure facilities and 'don't like the neighbours'. These answers suggest that if the quality of the housing and the environment in the area is improved then even more young people would want to stay.

Pupils were asked what kind of work they would like to do. The responses were highest for the categories of business, engineering and medicine. There were extremely few youngsters saying that they wanted to go into catering or tailoring. In practice the options for many youngsters when they leave school will not match up to their aspirations. Less will become doctors and more will end up in the family firm. However, the fact that the desire to work in the 'traditional' sectors of the area is so low, suggests that there will be profound changes in employment patterns for young people and especially for Bangladeshi students leaving education. Young Bangladeshis from Bethnal Green who leave school may still end up working in the area but it will increasingly be in the business service sector and less in the leather and restaurant trades.

## Education: together or apart?

The academic performance of pupils in Tower Hamlets has improved markedly in recent years, albeit from a very low base. The performance of schools with pupils from the Bethnal Green City Challenge area have improved their results at an even faster rate. This is partly explained by the fact that these schools have a high percentage of Bangladeshi pupils and the examintion results of Bangladeshi pupils have improved significantly over the last five years so that they now have the highest GCSE scores in the borough.

Over half of the pupils in Tower Hamlets are now Bangladeshi. Primary schools in the Bethnal Green City Challenge area have three-quarters of their places filled by Bangladeshi youngsters. The available evidence suggests that in Tower Hamlets, many schools are becoming overwhelmingly Bangladeshi or white. For example, a recent London Borough of Tower Hamlets report showed that one in five primary schools have fewer than ten per cent Bangladeshi pupils whilst almost as many have over 90 per cent of Bangladeshi origin.

The issue of parental choice plays an important part in any discussion of the make-up of a school. Many Bangladeshi parents may well want their children educated in an environment where they feel that there is less likelihood of racial harassment and where there would be more emphasis on their culture. Bangladeshi parents with daughters may well want them educated in a single sex school where peer group pressure respects traditional values.

In our School Students Survey, just under half (49 per cent) of the Bangladeshi girls expressed a preference for a single sex school. This compared to 22 per cent of Bangladeshi boys and 14 per cent of white

British girls. There is of course a problem in reconciling a situation where more girls than boys want single-sex as opposed to mixed schools.

From the point of view of the schools there are a number of implications of this trend. For example, one headteacher implied that a mono-cultural school was conducive to discipline and was welcomed from an administrative point of view. In addition, in terms of academic performance, it was also argued that achievement could be improved if pupils felt comfortable with the predominant culture and language of the pupils in the school. Some examples were cited that in a mixed environment, pupils from minority ethnic backgrounds who do poorly in school, appear to equate school experience with loss of their separate identity and resist following the rules of behaviour for academic success.

However, the majority of educationalists we spoke to expressed concern particularly with reference to the longer term implications. It was argued that segregation was leading to a low level of contact between children in different communities so hindering closer inter-community links. In the longer term, there is a real risk of the fragmentation of local communities along ethnic lines.

In the Bethnal Green area, we also find that many parents send their children outside school hours to a supplementary school. These schools have a number of different aims and provide tuition in heritage language, religious education and general educational enhancement. There has been a considerable expansion in these classes since 1992. This is partly due to the Section 11 Supplementary Schools Project and partly to the increased awareness amongst parents, pupils and educationalists of the benefits of such provision. The results obtained from pupils attending general study support supplementary schooling, such as Keen Students Supplementary School, demonstrate the benefits which can result. However, much of this provision is provided in a mono-cultural environment.

## Harassment

Minority communities in the East End have long been subjected to racial harassment and violence. Every so often these events catch the national media's attention as in the events which surrounded the election of a BNP councillor in Millwall and the extreme beating of a 17 year old Bangladeshi by a white gang.[10] However, even when media interest declines, the problems of harassment continue. This can occur at home, at school or on the streets.

The response can be passive or active. In a study of Bangladeshis in Camden,[11] it was found that respondents had begun to change aspects of their lives to avoid racial harassment. Nearly two-thirds of those interviewed had started to avoid going out at night, nearly a half had stopped their children from playing outside and a third had started to visit shops at certain times of the day. A more active response is being taken by some younger people. This involves groups of young Bangladeshi people taking a higher profile on the streets or on housing estates to obtain an improved level of safety.[12]

The events of 1993 appear to have led to a substantial increase in racial incidents and to a perception of increased racial harassment. Figures produced by the Metropolitan Police for the whole of Tower Hamlets shows that the level of substantiated racial incidents in the borough increased by 31 per cent between 1992 and 1993. (This took place against a rise of 17 per cent across the whole of the Metropolitan Police area.) The category of violence against the person and criminal damage registered significant increases. Unfortunately, more recent figures are not presently available. The perception of racial harassment in the Bethnal Green area can be gauged to some extent by the responses we obtained from our survey of residents. Whilst in early 1993, 41 per cent of Asian respondents perceived racial harassment as either a 'big problem' or 'something of a problem', by 1995 the percentage of Bangladeshis who answered in this way had increased significantly to 58 per cent.

In our study of young people, we found that 37 per cent of Bangladeshi youngsters in Tower Hamlets had experienced a racial problem. This was below the figure for black pupils in the borough (43 per cent) but above the percentage of white British schoolchildren who had faced a racial problem (32 per cent). Pupils were asked to comment on the nature of the problem. Amongst those replying and living in the Bethnal Green area, 84 per cent said that this was verbal abuse with 25 per cent saying that it involved physical violence. The issue of where these incidents took place is of relevance. Of those commenting, just under 20 per cent, noted problems taking place inside the school. Given the discussion earlier about the development of mono-cultural schools and the control of discipline, the distribution of pupils may affect the level of racial problems and the places where flash points may occur. Youth clubs, leisure facilities and the streets may then become the focus for any tensions. This highlights the important role of multi-cultural extra curricular activities to assist the development of inter-community links amongst young people in the area.

## Conclusion

At the beginning of this chapter, we asked two questions. What will the area look like in 20 years time and who will be living there? Secondly, are the Bangladeshi and white British communities moving together or apart? The one thing that we can say about forecasting the future is that almost certainly any predictions will be wrong. There are too many unknowns to be able to say what will happen. Still on the basis of what we know at present, we can make some informed guesses.

Almost certainly, the City will move eastward as far as Commercial Street. Office development will not exactly stop dead at this point but the large investment which has been made in improving the housing stock means that it is hard to contemplate large-scale redevelopment being allowed in the heart of the Bethnal Green area. The battle to retain the residential nature of the area has generally been won. It is more difficult to be sure what the economic structure of the area will be in 20 years time. The demise of the leather industry has been predicted before and, on the basis of what we know of the competitive pressures which are building up, it would be easy to say that its time has now come. But there is a resilience amongst those involved in the trade and the next generation of Bangladeshi business people may well take it into new directions. But the area already has a diversified economy with a significant level of business services. It is quite likely that many of the pupils presently at school will, in 20 years time, be running firms engaged in this growing sector rather than in the more traditional leather and restaurant trades.

Our discussions with developers and estate agents highlighted the changing image of the area as a residential location. More housing will be built in the area and the tenure profile will show increases in both owner-occupation and the housing association stock. In the immediate future, the owner-occupied homes will, in the main, be bought by youngish white British households without children. In the longer term, we would expect that more Bangladeshis will look to buy houses and flats in the area. Because of the size profile of the owner occupied stock, these will tend to be the smaller households. The larger households will continue to be dependent on the social housing sector and in particular the local authority stock. The demographic structure will mean that without significant new housebuilding of larger units, the level of overcrowding will get worse.

The demographic structure suggests that, for the next few years, the proportion of pupils who are of Bangladeshi origin is likely to increase. This will probably mean that there will be an increase in the number of schools which are predominantly mono-cultural. At the same time, on present trends the performance of Bangladeshi pupils will continue to outstrip those of the white British students. As the English language skills of pupils with Bangladeshi origins improve to a level where they become fully fluent, then research shows that their GCSE results will be significantly above the borough average and up to, and in many cases beyond, national standards. This is in spite of the disadvantages which overcrowded conditions in the home can cause in making it difficult to provide space for uninterrupted study.

On present trends, the overall education profile of the population is likely to improve. The incoming white British households are well qualified and are obtaining jobs to match their education profile. Many more Bangladeshi young people are now obtaining A levels and degrees. The extent to which these increased educational achievements of the Bangladeshi population can be translated into improved earning power will be one of the crucial issues in the coming years.

If we turn to the second of the questions, we see that at a superficial level the two communities appear to be moving apart. There is a growing divergence in the tenure profile of the two communities and an increasing tendency to mono-cultural education. Bangladeshi adults and pupils perceived a high level of racial harassment in the area. On the other side of the coin, Bangladeshi households are now to be found in a far greater number of housing estates than was the case 20 years ago. There is far greater interaction across a range of social and leisure activities. Bangladeshi representation in the political process has increased substantially. Bangladeshi women are now becoming involved in political mobilisation through a range of local organisations. Much useful work on developing inter-community relations has been carried out through the Bethnal Green City Challenge programme.

The present residents of Bethnal Green share with their predecessors high aspirations for the future. As the economic situation for many improves they will also have to face the decision which different immigrant communities have pondered, on whether to move or stay in the area. In the past, the answer has been to move. The improved living environment in Bethnal Green suggests that the outward drift of the Bangladeshi community may be slower. This has implications not only for the community itself but also for the future social and economic structure of this intriguing area.

**Notes**

---

[1] LEPU, *Living in Bethnal Green: A Survey of Residents in the Bethnal Green City Challenge Area*, London, South Bank University, 1995.

[2] SCPR, *The Residents of Bethnal Green, Their Characteristics and Views*, London, Social and Community Planning and Research (35 Northampton Square, London EC1), 1994.

[3] LEPU, *School Student Survey Tower Hamlets*, London, South Bank University, 1995.

[4] LEPU, *Living in Bethnal*, op.cit.

[5] C. Foreman, *Spitalfields: A Battle for Land*, London, Hilary Shipman, 1989.

[6] Ibid., see Chapter 3.

[7] Ibid., p. 63.

[8] London Borough of Tower Hamlets, *Housing Strategy and HIP Bid*, London 1995/96.

[9] LEPU, *School Student Survey*, op.cit.

[10] M. Keith, 'Making the Street Visible: Placing Racial Violence in Context', *New Community*, 21(4), 1995, pp. 551-65.

[11] London Borough of Camden and the Institute of Education, *Camden Bangladeshi Residents Survey*, London, 1996.

[12] Keith, op.cit.

# 9 The 'Return' of the Jews into London

*Stanley Waterman*

About 10 years ago, I did some collaborative work with Barry Kosmin who was then the Director of Research at the Board of Deputies of British Jews. We produced a series of papers that dealt mostly with the Jewish community in the United Kingdom in general, and with the Jews of north-west London, in particular.[1] The work that we did was simultaneously satisfying and frustrating.

The satisfaction was twofold. On the one hand, we were able to produce and analyze spatial data on a population that had been ignored to a large extent; at the same time, we were able to ask a series of questions about the migration patterns of Jews and how they form new communities. The frustration was that we were not able to provide adequate answers to the questions that we asked because we lacked the right type of data. The data that we analysed were only surrogates for real data. We used the electoral roll and 'distinctive Jewish names' as our tools. The data were static, limited to a single period in time only. We used voting data that had been updated in February 1985 and we linked it to the 1981 population census. Moreover, much of what we wrote was speculative. Although we talked about trends in the distribution of Jewish population in London, and hypothesised about what might happen in the future, we really did not know too much about migration intentions or perceptions.

Such was the nature of the constraints under which we worked then. We had no funds to carry out surveys to generate data on what I was really interested in at the time, namely, residential change and the migration of

Jews and Jewish neighbourhoods within and throughout the metropolis. In particular, I was interested in three things. First, in what ways did perceptions differ as to what constituted a Jewish (ethnic) neighbourhood from within and without, i.e. as perceived by the Jews (ethnic group members) themselves as compared with outside observers?[2] Secondly, why was there a persistent tendency for Jews, when migrating, to continue to seek Jewish ethnic environments, that is, why they continued to cluster.[3] Closely related to this was the question of by what process is a new ethnic area formed?[4]

In this short essay, I would like to discuss the residential patterns and processes of Jews in the Greater London area and in the zone immediately beyond this, at the end of the 20th century. In doing this, I would like to make some mention of some ideas to be found in the literature on the geography of migration in general. Many of the ideas pertaining to the Jews in Greater London receive only oblique reference in the general migration literature, because much of this literature still deals with (a) international migration, and (b) first migration rather than return migration.[5] True, there is a growing body of literature in urban geography and sociology that deals with changing residential patterns in cities and metropolitan areas, but much of this relates to the analysis of census data which are heavily biased by the nature of the data that the census generates.[6] These data are not necessarily those that social scientists interested in ethnic migration within cities find most useful. In the case of the Jews in Britain, no such data exist, as data on neither religious nor ethnic affiliation, the two categories under which one could expect to find figures relating to Jews, are collected.

## Migration

The criticism of the migration data relating to international migration and first migration is particularly true of the historical literature of which the study of the migrant in his new land is an interesting element. The allegorical bias of the historical literature is obviously less marked in the case of the social sciences, in which demographers, geographers, and sociologists obviously have their own particular disciplinary agendas to play out, but these two biases nevertheless persist there, too, if in a rather different way.[7]

In terms of international migration, it is still a truism that most people stay put and do not migrate at all, so that migrants are only a small minority of the world's population. Of those who do move, most stay at their original destinations or move on somewhere else (another cliché about migration is that once the bonds tying a person to a place have been loosened, it is much easier to move again). However, only a small proportion return to their places of origin, and fewer still return to the places from which their parents and more distant forebears set out. There are, of course, exceptions. The literature on, say, Italian return migration is quite extensive. But then those Italian migrants that returned to Italy after, say, 30 or 40 years in the USA or Argentina, were different from most previous modern-day migrants at the outset, in that their original intention in moving was always to return home at the end of whatever period they planned to stay.[8]

One of the features of modern-day migration is the great flexibility experienced by the migrant. Whereas migrations that preceded the second half of the 20th century were surface-based migrations, those since 1950, especially migration to the developed countries, has been by air, and the advent of cheap jet transport has served to make migration much less permanent and daunting, much more of a transient process, than in the past. The physical possibility of returning home is much more *realisable* today than ever before. Notwithstanding this, most migrants stay in their country of destination, and as they move upwards socially, many move on from their areas of first settlement.

In cases in which no return migration to the country of origin has occurred, there has been a truncation of the migration chain. This truncation might occur when there are inherent difficulties, such as those occurring as a result of distance and cost, or disruptions at the point of origin, making return impossible or worst or at best unattractive. This was the case in international migrations in times past, and still true today for international migrations involving movement of people from Less Developed Countries to the West and the urbanisation movement from village to town in the Third World.

But this essay, although related to ideas, concepts, and events in international migration, is concerned with a form of migration that has been prevalent since the Industrial Revolution in particular. Internal migration takes place within individual states and has become part of 'modern' living. Moreover, some states have often been more reticent or inept at collecting data on internal migration than on international migrants. Until the 20th century, internal migration from rural areas to urban areas represented the principal flow of internal migrants. As the immigrants began to sort themselves out after their arrival in the towns and cities, redistribution (both within the state and the city or town of first settlement) became more important. From the advent of cheap suburban railways in the last century and the private automobile throughout this, the predominant area of research on internal migration has been concerned with suburbanization and the development of new towns.

More recently, one of the types of move to have attracted attention is the tendency for some people to seek to reside closer to the city centre. This is often seen as a life-cycle event, part of the flux of modern life where young families seek a house in the suburbs, and younger singles and older couples may seek a central location. Of course, this is very general and there are always those who cannot or do not wish to move to the suburbs or central city. Some, such as people in middle-age who leave the metropolitan area altogether to live in the country or young marrieds with small families who choose to live as near as possible to the centre of the city, buck the trend completely. However, the census provides little data to study these trends adequately, and there is much reliance on the generation of data from survey material or from qualitative observations.

**London, the Jews and intra-metropolitan migration**

Several questions need to be addressed when investigating current trends among the residential patterns of the Jews of London, and in particular the issue of return migration, or the tendency for some households to move back towards central London from the suburbs. The first is the issue of '*Where is London?*' This confronts us with an immediate problem. If we wish to learn something about the people who went out to live in the suburbs and then have moved back into town, we must try to define what is meant by London and its suburbs. The second issue deals with '*Who is a Jew?*' This is hardly less vexing. In particular, as intermarriage with, and assimilation into, the general community becomes more marked and easier to achieve for those who desire it, some people who are not fully recognized by the orthodox Jewish authorities as Jewish enter the community by dint of marriage and the identity they give to their households after marriage; others, who are Jews according to *halachah*, Jewish orthodox laws and customs, effectively leave the community. Who should be counted? Finally, assuming that adequate answers can be provided for these two questions (and it is doubtful that they can; the debates continue), a third issue looms. *How are data acquired on the Jews, as the Census does not count Jews as such?* Earlier work used an ethnic names and/or data from the electoral register, but though this was useful at the time, it was not regarded as satisfactory even then, just the best that could be achieved given the limitations of the research.[9] In the 1990s, better data are available from the electoral register. Using >400 names identified as distinctively Jewish, it is possible to estimate with a higher degree of accuracy than before the proportion of Jews living in given areas. The method is not foolproof, just an improvement - a development - on earlier work.

Overall, the movement of people to the suburbs can be seen as the growth and expansion of the original concentration. It may well be a diluted concentration but what develops is nevertheless a concentration, for migration is hardly ever a random process. Jews, like all other movers, but especially like other ethnic minority movers, tend to restrict their field of choice to a limited number of areas. When they spread out from the areas of first settlement in the East End, they moved into areas like Hackney and Dalston; later, more wealthy Jews moved into the north-western sector, into St. John's Wood and Hampstead. With the arrival of the Northern Line of the Underground Railway in 1907, there was migration to Golders Green, with a further outward movement towards Finchley and Hendon; the line eventually reached Edgware in 1926 and Jewish high holy day services were reported by the end of the decade. After the Second World War, there was a leapfrogging as far as the outer suburb of Edgware from which there was a more gradual movement into Stanmore and Pinner, and outside the Green Belt, into Bushey, Elstree, Borehamwood and Radlett. After the war, there was an increase in the pace of movement outwards from the community that remained in the East End into nearby outer suburban areas in northeast London, centred on Ilford, a Jewish counterpart to the populations reported by Young and Willmott,[10] with the important difference that the Jewish migration was into private housing whereas Young and Willmott's populations were housed in the public sector (Figure 1).

It is somewhat illogical to think of people who moved to Edgware or Stanmore in the 1930s or after the Second World War as living in anywhere but London, just as in the same way, their children and grandchildren moved a few kilometres further down the road to Bushey, Elstree, Borehamwood and Radlett. They remained Londoners, but they were Londoners of a different kind. There was no appreciable psychological migration and the frame of reference was still London, certainly until the mid-1970s. Perhaps because of their attachment to community, perhaps more precisely to community institutions and their continuing need to maintain contacts with ethnic 'roof' institutions that were focused on London proper, their move to the suburbs was less marked, perhaps even less permanent, than those migrants who were part of the secular majority. After all, a migrant to the suburbs who is no longer in need of ties to the centre of origin, can transform much more completely into a new suburban identity than one who still requires a kosher butcher, a Jewish school, and other community facilities.

It was their lifestyles that became what we term 'suburban'. In other words, they spent much of their time in cars, ferrying children from one activity to another as well as for shopping and travelling for leisure purposes. They became 'more affluent', or at least their ways of life appeared to become more affluent; in other words they achieved a lifestyle that began to approach that of the so-called 'American Dream' - a house, two cars, a double-garage in which to park them.[11] Their electoral behaviour, too, changed during this transformation from 'urban' to 'suburban', and erstwhile Labour supporters became Tories, if not of the 'true-blue' variety, then of the 'blue-and-white' kind, especially during the Thatcher era, with the Prime Minister herself representing Finchley, an Outer London constituency with a sizeable proportion of Jews, though far from being the 'most Jewish' area in London, a title today contested by Golders Green, Edgware, and Ilford. But the point to be stressed at this juncture is that these migrant Jews, and their children and grandchildren who became the archetypal suburbanites, have never really left London.

First of all, the general perception of what constitutes London has changed over the years. Over the past two centuries, definitions of London have changed. Small villages were captured by suburban ribbon development as the city spread out along its railway lines from the 1840s, and later were engulfed by the rapid, blanket spread of the metropolis. Just over a hundred years ago, the distinction was made (because circumstances demanded it) between the City of London and the Metropolitan County. The old London County Council created in 1889 endured as a semi-official version of London for about 80 years until it was replaced by another geographical administrative unit, the Greater London Council, in 1964. But, as with other redistributions of political power, that of the 1960s did no more than simply follow a population trend that had already occurred in the preceding decades. In various studies on the London region carried out from the mid-1960s to the late-1970s, planners were actually looking at much more extensive regions for instance, the South-East that were really euphemisms for a more extensive London. People living in places like Luton, Cambridge, Colchester and Ipswich that were sizeable and political separate local authorities were considered to be on the outer reaches of a Greater London, as people could commute (and many did) within a hour to an hour and a half from workplaces in London. There was a general understanding that the functional boundaries of a Greater London had extended far beyond the administrative boundaries of even the most liberal attempt to govern London as a unit or as a federation covering a much more extensive journey-to-work area.

However, we have to consider the Jewish population that migrated to the outer boroughs of Greater London and beyond - the people in Edgware and Stanmore and Redbridge, and those beyond, in Bushey, Borehamwood, Elstree and Radlett.[12] Most never really regarded themselves as anything but Londoners, even though they were 20 to 30 kilometres from the city and from the historical core of Jewish London in the East End, and even 15 kilometres from such secondary centres as Hendon and Golders Green. Technically, they were migrants, people who had made a move from one place of permanent residence to another. Yet, although they lived in the 'sticks' beyond London proper and were thus physically migrants, they continued to use the city - both the more strictly urban area as well as the metropolis as a whole - on a daily basis. In this respect, they were different from many other similar migrants, other people who up and leave their homes, not to move abroad, and as a consequence, change the pattern of their lives.[13]

Most of the Jewish migrants to the outer suburbs and exurbs continued to work and shop in London. Cultural life was in the city, at least for those who were not locked into their armchairs watching TV and videos. Theatre and music and other forms of 'high' culture remained in the city, and circulation patterns took this into consideration. In many cases, their children continued to be sent to schools in London, and had Haberdasher's Askes School not moved out to Elstree, the Jewish pupils who form a substantial proportion of the roll there would undoubtedly have continued to come into the city just as the children who attend City of London, University College, and South Hampstead schools do, as well as the many children attending Jewish primary schools and secondary schools such as JFS in Camden and the strictly orthodox Hasmonean schools for boys and girls in Barnet.

*London: the promised land?*

Modern British Jewry has always been concentrated in London.[14] That is an historical fact. If anything, this trend has become more marked over the years. Approximately two-thirds of those identifying as Jews in one way or another are in Greater London, and about two-thirds of all deaths and burials are registered in the capital. Almost all the Jewish institutions in Britain are centred on London, and most nonconformist brands of Judaism seem to have a firmer footing in London than elsewhere, whether Masorti (Conservative), Reform, or Liberal Jewish synagogues and community institutions. Thus, from every point of view, London has always been central to Jewish life.

This centrality of London has probably been truer for Jews than for most other ethnic groups.[15] The Irish, the Afro-Caribbeans, and the South Asians are much less centrally attached to London than are the Jews, and all those groups are less concentrated in the capital than the Jews.[16] Only the Bangladeshis, with their current concentration in the historical area of first Jewish settlement in the East End, are more highly concentrated within the capital than the Jews.

Whereas most population estimates for British Jewry have shown that there has been a constant decline from a high in the early 1950s (the estimates for then were probably unrealistically high), the decline in London has been much less sharp than in the rest of the country.[17] The only other centre in the United Kingdom that has managed more or less to retain its numbers is Manchester.[18]

This is because London has remained the main target for migrant Jews from all over the country *and* from abroad. Whereas Manchester has added to its numbers primarily by absorbing population from northern British provincial centres that have declined substantially, such as Glasgow, Liverpool, Leeds, and Dublin, London has attracted its Jewish migrants from all these places and from Manchester itself, as well as from centres to the south of Manchester. Moreover, a good proportion of the Manchester growth has been related to the in-migration of orthodox Jews from the other centres, thus making Manchester into a place of 'refuge and reconstitution' for the so-called ultra-Orthodox or *Haredi* Jews, a factor that makes it less attractive to more secular Jews, and adding to the long-standing differences between the Jewish communities in North and South Manchester.

London, on the other hand, has managed to retain a more cosmopolitan atmosphere in which different strains of Jewish practice and customs can thrive. It attracted Jews of all varieties - ultra-Orthodox, mainstream Ashkenazi Orthodox, other Jewish varietals, secular Jews - the whole gamut. More likely than not, it is the overall size of London that permits this; the vast area covered by the metropolis means that it is large enough to sustain a variety of communities so that even if they do antagonise one another, they are nevertheless strong enough to co-exist. There is very simply sufficient geographical space to permit coexistence.

**Foreign Jews in the 1970s and beyond**

London has continued to be a source of attraction to many of the immigrants coming to Britain. For instance, it is the main centre of attraction for immigrants from South Africa and the Middle East. It is these factors, probably more than anything else, that has enabled London to continue to attract Jewish immigrants from abroad. Far from having dried up, Jews still come to London. They no longer arrive in the numbers that were common in the three decades preceding the First World War, though current streams might resemble that of the 1930s when Jews from central Europe arrived as refugees from Hitler's invasions and atrocities. Moreover, there should be no doubting that such a stream of migration still exists today. It does exist, and it comes primarily from two sources, Israel and South Africa, and to a lesser extent from North America and Europe.

It is hard to know exactly how many Israelis there are in the United Kingdom because of the questions asked on the census; in the 1991 census there were around 16,000 Israeli-born of whom three-quarters lived in London. However, many Israelis are not Israeli-born, so that in a paper ten years ago, Kosmin and Waterman estimated that this figure underestimated the number of actual Israelis by a factor of 2.57.[19] Thus, there is more likely to be something like 40,000 Israelis in the United Kingdom, of whom around 30,000 are in London. The Israelis simply exaggerate the tendency for Jews, already observed among local British community, to prefer London to other places in the country as a place of residence. This preference for the capital is even more marked among the South Africans; one estimate for the South African Jewish population suggests that well over 80 percent of South African Jews who have migrated to the United Kingdom in the past 30 years have chosen to base themselves in London.[20]

In many ways, Jewish migrants who come to London - whether from within the United Kingdom or from outside - have reached a 'point of no return'. In London, they can, if they choose, remain fully Jewish at home and in a Jewish community of their choosing, yet interact with the general community with ease. In other words, they can be Jewish privately and while publicly, they are cosmopolitan.[21] Equally easily, if they so choose, they can disperse among the general community with greater facility than anywhere else in the country. Moreover, they are unlikely to return to their points of origin even though they may consider Glasgow, or Birmingham or Leeds to be 'home'. There is little to attract a London in-migrant back to his original home in the provinces, and on the few occasions when such return migration occurs, it is more likely to be because of some negative factor such as illness, or bankruptcy, where family ties may make recovery easier than in the relative anonymity of London.

The greater propensity observable among first-time migrants to become migrants again generally does not mean that return migration will occur. It refers rather to later migrations to other places. Comparing Israelis and South African Jewish migrants in London, the Israelis are the more likely of the two to engage in return migration than the South Africans, if only because Israeli identity and its Zionist roots have laid so much stress on immigration to Israel *(Aliyah)* that emigration - leaving Israel *(Yeridah)* - used to be seen as something approaching treason. As a consequence, *most* Israeli emigrants will tell you that they still intend to return to Israel or (if things are either too difficult or comfortable to permit that), hope that their children will. Very few, if any, of the South Africans will echo those sentiments.[22]

One of the features shared by both the Israelis and the South Africans in Greater London is that they share less in the suburban tendencies that we have been able to observe among British Jews in the past six decades. Not having been part of the British Jewish community prior to their arrival, they have been less hindered by the distribution of the existing Jewish community than have Jews migrating into London from the provinces. In fact, many, though not all, of both the Israeli and South African immigrants have had only minimal connections with the organized community based on synagogue affiliation, and their desire for contacts with other Jews is motivated more by ethnic affiliation than anything based purely on religion. This, of course, applies less to those Jewish immigrants who are strictly orthodox, and are thus much more constrained by physical distance and proximity to other Jews.

As a consequence, we are more likely to find greater proportions of South African and Israeli immigrant Jews close to central London than for the Jewish population of London as a whole. Areas such as Golders Green and Hampstead have become popular centres attracting immigrant Jews in the 1980s and 1990s. In addition, there are some indications that some of these immigrants choose to relocate in parts of the metropolis that have only small Jewish populations, perhaps after initially locating fairly close to existing Jewish centres of population. However, this locational behaviour on the part of the Israelis and the South Africans who are already more London-oriented than the Jewish population as a whole, simply provides an example of a trend that can also be recognized among the native British Jews, namely a move back into central areas from the suburbs. This movement is reflected in the revival of Jewish life in the northwest sector of London, between Regent's Park and Golders Green, as can be seen by the revival of several of the synagogues in the area.

The South Hampstead Synagogue (part of the United Synagogue) and the Belsize Square Liberal Synagogue (an independent synagogue established in the 1930s by German refugees from Berlin), were both in an advanced state of decline a decade ago, afflicted by outmigration to the suburbs and the ageing and deaths of many of their respective founder-members. In 1996, they are thriving communities with memberships of over 1,000 each. Each is led by a rabbi with very positive views on expanding their respective communities, themselves immigrants from Johannesburg and Melbourne, respectively, and each synagogue has an extensive outreach programme.

However, neither of these two communities could have succeeded without an appropriate 'clientele' living in the area, especially in the case of South Hampstead with its orthodox affiliation and Hassidic rabbi. This population is living mainly in reconverted and purpose-built flats and houses in these areas that command high property prices. The South Africans (and to a lesser extent, the Israelis) are prominent amongst these communities, but they are by no means the predominant elements among the newcomers that have moved into inner London during the past decade.

The Jewish population of areas such as Hampstead, West Hampstead and Belsize Park comprise mostly small households. It is a broad mixture. There is an older population comprising what remains of the original membership of the synagogues in the area, and others. In addition to this declining population, there are those younger people, either singles, couples, or those with small and young families who have moved back in towards the city, having spent their youth in the suburbs. They have traded space for convenience so as to be closer to work and to leisure facilities offered by the West End; others have never in fact left the area and are the children of families who have lived in the area for two or three generations, but who stay for more or less the same reasons as those who have moved in. Most of these young households comprise professionals - doctors, dentists, lawyers, and members of ancillary professions, as well as people in advertising, journalism, radio and television, and retailing. Many of those who have moved back into the centre of the metropolis probably only saw their sojourn in the suburbs as a temporary venture, even if it lasted 25-30 years.

The renaissance of these two established synagogues is not a one-off event, and is being repeated, albeit on a more modest scale in other centrally located London communities, such as the West End-Marble Arch synagogue and in St. John's Wood. And, if one considers that synagogue membership accounts for perhaps two-thirds to three-quarters of the Jewish population, and that Jews who do not belong to an established community are probably less in need of ethnic facilities, then it is likely that this revival of inner city communities is considerably larger than it appears on the surface.

## Conclusion

However, all this needs to be put in some perspective. Just as a single sparrow does not necessarily herald the onset of spring, the revival of three or four declining synagogues does not mean that new Jewish communities are springing up throughout inner London. This is very much a life-cycle phenomenon, brought about as some more affluent persons find locations to suit what they desire and can afford. For the majority of the Jewish population, whether those comparatively strapped by mortgages and children and the desire for a relatively large living space, or for those with even larger families who need to live in a strong and vibrant community, movement towards the centre of the metropolis is not a viable alternative to their current lifestyles; in fact, it is not a consideration at all. In these cases, the draw of the next suburbs outward is as strong as it was two and three generations ago.

The resurrection of Jewish life in inner northwest London needs to be placed in proper perspective. The numbers and proportions of Jews living in these areas are both absolutely and proportionately small when compared with other areas in which there is a recognisably strong Jewish residential presence. Table 1 shows this to be the case. The figures for a number of London Postal Areas were calculated for those six-digit postcodes in which there was at least one household carrying a recognizable Jewish name. The second column of the Table gives the number of such households in that *subset* of postcodes. The third column shows the number of households with a recognisably Jewish name, and the fourth expresses this as a percentage of households in the postcode sub-set. The final column estimates the percentage Jewish population in this sub-set of postcodes, showing a figure for the areas of Jewish concentration within that larger postal area.

**Table 1: Approximate percentage of Jews in the population of selected postal areas of London (inner London shaded)**

| Postal area | No. of households in Postcode sub-set | No. of households with Jewish names | Percent with Jewish names | Approx. % Jewish in Postcode sub-set |
|---|---|---|---|---|
| E1 | 5,441 | 130 | 2.4 | 16.9 |
| HA5 | 4,513 | 112 | 2.5 | 17.5 |
| HA7 | 6,587 | 341 | 5.2 | 36.5 |
| HA8 | 9,566 | 590 | 6.2 | 43.5 |
| IG | 4,093 | 96 | 2.3 | 16.6 |
| N16 | 12,307 | 513 | 4.2 | 29.4 |
| N2 | 4,905 | 259 | 5.3 | 37.3 |
| N3 | 6,402 | 241 | 3.8 | 26.6 |
| NW11 | 10,371 | 700 | 6.7 | 47.7 |
| NW4 | 7,942 | 612 | 7.7 | 54.4 |
| NW6 | 7,940 | 190 | 2.4 | 16.9 |
| NW8 | 3,906 | 125 | 3.2 | 22.6 |
| NW3 | 11,464 | 355 | 3.1 | 21.9 |

Source: CACI Ltd. Information Services, Market Analysis and Information Sevices: London. Derived from data supplied to Jewish Policy Research in connection with the survey on Social and Political Attitudes of British Jews, 1994.

Clearly, areas such as Edgware, Ilford, Golders Green, Hendon, Hampstead Garden Suburb, and even Finchley are more heavily Jewish, both in numbers and in proportion of the total population, than any of the inner London areas shown shaded in the Table. Moreover, the rebirth of communities in Inner London has been highly selective. There has been no Jewish sentimentality leading to serious attempts to resettle former Jewish areas of historical significance such as Whitechapel and Spitalfields. These are associated with Jewish history in London and not with Jewish futures. They may be geographically close to the City where many Jews work, the spatial proximity is no longer a good reason for choosing a place of residence when the space is associated with economic and social decline. Similarly, there has not been any substantial migration south of the Thames. The decision to move back towards the centre is no more and no less than a rational choice for those who can afford it and should be seen in that light.

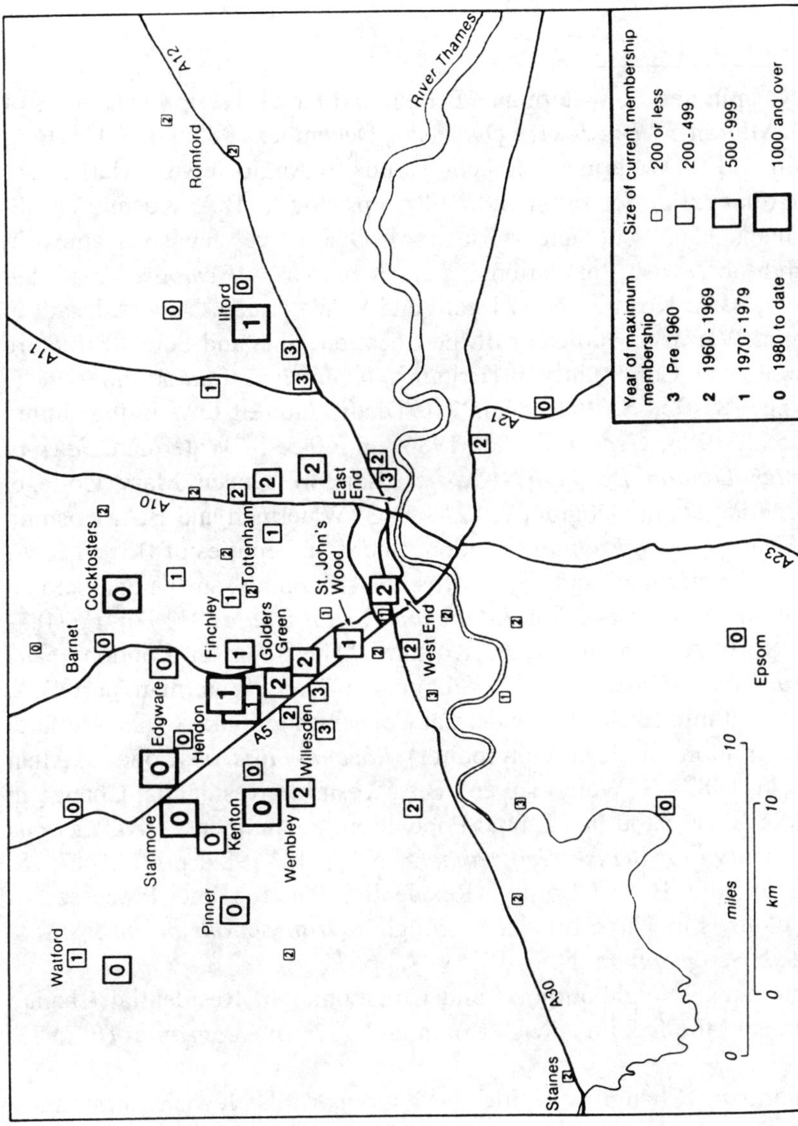


**Figure 1: Current size and periods of maximum membership of the United Synagogue**

**Notes**

---

[1] B.A. Kosmin and S. Waterman, 'Britain and Israel: Reciprocal Flows of Jewish Migrants', *The Jewish Quarterly*, December 1985, pp. 7-11; B.A. Kosmin and S. Waterman, 'Recent Trends in Anglo-Jewish Marriages', *Jewish Journal of Sociology*, 28, 1986, pp. 49-57; B.A. Kosmin and S. Waterman, 'The Use and Misuse of Distinctive Jewish Names in Research on Jewish Populations', *Papers in Jewish Demography*, 1989, pp. 1-10; B.A. Kosmin, N. Grizzard and S. Waterman, 'Jewish Death in the Great War as an Indicator of the Location, Size and Social Structure of the Jewish Community in Britain', *Immigrants and Minorities*, 5, 1986, pp. 181-92; S. Waterman, 'The Distribution of Jews in the United Kingdom', 1984, *Geography* 71, 1986, pp. 60-5; S. Waterman, *Jews in an Outer London Borough - Barnet*, London, Queen Mary College, Research Papers in Geography, 1, 1989; S. Waterman and B.A. Kosmin, *British Jewry in the Eighties*, London, Board of Deputies of British Jews, 1986; S. Waterman and B.A. Kosmin, Mapping an Unenumerated Population - Jews in London, *Ethnic and Racial Studies* 9, 1986, pp. 484-501; S. Waterman and B.A. Kosmin, 'The Jews in London', *The Geographical Magazine* 58, 1986, pp. 21-7; S. Waterman and B.A. Kosmin, 'Ethnic Identity, Residential Concentration and Social Welfare: Jews in London', in P. Jackson (editor), *Race and Racism*, London, Allen & Unwin, 1987; S. Waterman and B.A. Kosmin, 'Residential Change in a Middle-Class Suburban Ethnic Population: a Comment', *Transactions of the Institute of British Geographers* (N.S.), 12, 1987, pp. 111-17; S. Waterman and B.A. Kosmin, 'Residential Patterns and Processes: a Study of Jews in Three London Boroughs', *Transactions of the Institute of British Geographers* (N.S.) 13, 1988, pp. 75-91.

[2] S. Waterman, 'Neighbourhood and Community in Residential Change Decisions in the Dublin Jewish Community', *Irish Geography* 16, 1983, pp. 55-68.

[3] S. Waterman, 'Changing Residential Patterns of the Jewish Community in Dublin', *Irish Geography* 14, 1981, pp. 41-50, and Waterman 'Neighbourhood and Community'.

[4] K.N. Conzen, 'Immigrants, Immigrant Neighborhoods and Ethnic Identity', *Journal of American History* 66, 1979, pp. 603-15, and Waterman, *Jews in an Outer London Borough*.

5 See W.A.V. Clark, *Human Migration*, Beverly Hills, Ca., Sage Publications, 1986; D. Henderson, 'International Migration: Appraising Current Policies', *International Affairs* 70, 1994, pp. 93-110 and E.S. Lee, 'A Theory of Migration', *Demography* 3, 1996, pp. 47-67.

6 W.A.V. Clark, 'Comparing Cross-Sectional and Longitudinal Analyses of Residential Mobility and Migration', *Environment and Planning 'A'* 24, 1992, pp. 1291-302, and C. Hamnett, 'The Relationship Between Residential Migration and Housing Tenure in London 1971-81: A Longitudinal Analysis', *Environment and Planning 'A'* 23, 1991, pp. 1147-62.

7 S. Waterman and M. Schmool, 'The Jewish Immigrant Experience in Britain', in R. King, P. White and J. Connell (editors), *Writing Across Worlds: Literature and Migration*, London, Routledge, 1995.

8 R. King, *Il Ritorno In Patria*, Durham: Occasional Publications, University of Durham, Department of Geography, New Series 23, 1988.

9 Kosmin and Waterman, 'The Use and Misuse of Distinctive Jewish Names', and Waterman and Kosmin, 'Mapping an Unenumerated'.

10 M. Young and P. Willmott, *Family and Kinship in East London*, London, Routledge and Kegan Paul, 1957.

11 S. Waterman, 'The Geographic Expansion of Jewish Communities and its Implication for Social Cohesion and Community Organisation', in S. Della Pergola and L. Cohen (editors), *World Jewish Population: Trends and Policies*, Jerusalem, Institute of Contemporary Jewry, Hebrew University of Jerusalem, 1992, pp. 106-11.

12 D. Graham, *The Jewish Effect: An Analysis of Radlett's Jewish Community*, London, Independent Geographical Project, Department of Geography, London School of Economics, 1996.

13 Waterman, *Jews in an Outer London Borough.*

14 Waterman and Kosmin, *British Jewry in the Eighties*, and Waterman and Kosmin, *The Jews in London.*

15 Many British Jews do not take to being called an ethnic group because of the pejorative associations that the name conjures up. Many like to be closely associated with the majority culture, and thus not reminded of their group origins. Others prefer to dissociate themselves from the majority culture on the basis of their religious beliefs and practices rather than just a unique history (or historical associations), although arguably, it is these very beliefs and practices that make them a distinct ethnic group. But that is another issue entirely.

[16] D. Owen, 'Ethnicity in the 1991 Census', in D. Coleman and J. Salt (editors), *Size, Structure and Growth of the Ethnic Minority Popultions, Vol. 1, Demographic Characteristics of the Ethnic Minority Populations*, London, HMSO, 1996.

[17] See S.J. Prais and M. Schmool, 'The Size and Structure of the Anglo-Jewish Population, 1960-65' in *Jewish Journal of Sociology* 10, 1968, pp. 5-34; S. Haberman, B.A. Kosmin and C. Levy, 'Mortality Patterns of British Jews 1975-79: Insights and Applications for the Size and Structure of British Jewry', *Journal of the Royal Statistical Society*, A, 146, 1983, pp. 294-310, and S. Haberman and M. Schmool, 'Estimates of the British Jewish Population, 1984-88', *Journal of the Royal Statistical Society*, A, 158, 1995, pp. 547-62.

[18] Waterman and Kosmin, *British Jewry in the Eighties*.

[19] Kosmin and Waterman, 'Britain and Israel'.

[20] S. Haas, 'Similarities Between General Immigration Experience and Particular Experiences of South African Jews in the United Kingdom' (unpublished MS).

[21] See S. Miller, M. Schmool and A. Lerman, *Social and Political Attitudes of British Jews: Some Key Findings of the JPR Survey*, London, Institute for Jewish Policy Research, 1996.

[22] S. Haas, 'Similarities Between General Immigration Experience'.

# Index